MUD
FLATS
AND
FISH
CAMPS

800 MILES AROUND
ALASKA'S COOK INLET

ERIN McKITTRICK

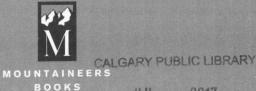

MOUNTAINEERS
BOOKS

For Katmai, Lituya, and the unwritten future.

Mountaineers Books is the publishing division of The Mountaineers, an organization founded in 1906 and dedicated to the exploration, preservation, and enjoyment of outdoor and wilderness areas.

MOUNTAINEERS BOOKS

1001 SW Klickitat Way, Suite 201 • Seattle, WA 98134
800.553.4453 • www.mountaineersbooks.org

Printed in the United States of America
Distributed in the United Kingdom by Cordee, www.cordee.co.uk
20 19 18 17   1 2 3 4 5

Copyeditor: Amy Smith Bell
Design and layout: Heidi Smets Graphic Design
Cartographer: Bretwood "Hig" Higman
Cover photograph: *Fingers of muddy sand flow down the beach in a tiny trickle.*
Back cover photograph: *A friend joins us for a piece of the journey, paddling the sometimes treacherous waters of Turnagain Arm.*

Library of Congress Cataloging-in-Publication Data
Names: McKittrick, Erin, author.
Title: Mudflats and fish camps : 800 miles around Alaska's Cook Inlet / Erin McKittrick.
Description: Seattle, WA : Mountaineers Books, [2017] | Includes bibliographical references.
Identifiers: LCCN 2016035229| ISBN 9781680510188 (pbk.) | ISBN 9781680510195 (ebook)
Subjects: LCSH: McKittrick, Erin—Travel—Alaska—Cook Inlet (Region) | Cook Inlet Region (Alaska)—Description and travel.
Classification: LCC F912.C6 M34 2014 | DDC 551.46/1434—dc23
LC record available at https://lccn.loc.gov/2016035229

Mountaineers Books titles may be purchased for corporate, educational, or other promotional sales, and our authors are available for a wide range of events. For information on special discounts or booking an author, contact our customer service at 800-553-4453 or mbooks@mountaineersbooks.org.

 Printed on recycled paper

ISBN (paperback): 978-1-68051-018-8
ISBN (ebook): 978-1-68051-019-5

CONTENTS

PROLOGUE

CAPTAIN COOK'S INLET

Cook Inlet is a hook-shaped silt-brown waterway, slicing deep into the heart of Alaska. On Captain James Cook's map, it resembles the head of a rabbit. Augustine Volcano forms the dot of an eye, and the rabbit's ears stretch all the way to Anchorage. It's the deepest part of an ice-carved valley, ringed by mountains and glaciers, cradling the urban and the wild. People followed the melting ice, maybe slowly, or maybe arriving when the glaciers were just starting to draw back into high mountain valleys, leaving behind scoured slopes of rock, gravel plains dotted with white dryas fluff and pink river beauty flowers, waters still choked with ice. Families may have pulled up on its beaches in small boats, looking for new territory. At the head of the inlet, there are tools that could be ten thousand years old. Nearer the mouth, bits of charcoal have been dated at eight thousand years old. There may be older sites, buried beneath the sea or under earth that no one has ever dug up.

Archaeologists call those first explorers "traditions": the Ocean Bay tradition, the Arctic Small Tool tradition, the Marine Kachemak tradition, the Alutiiq, the Dena'ina. These explorers discovered new territory—maybe uninhabited, maybe not—then moved in for centuries or millennia, leaving their own particular tools and architecture behind. We do know that thousands of years later, the mouth of Cook Inlet was the first part that anyone wrote about. Russian explorers reached Alaska in 1741, and in the decades that followed, their fur hunting camps were scattered across the Aleutians, spreading eastward along the coast. Their forts hadn't quite reached Cook Inlet when Captain Cook sailed around this corner in 1778, approaching from the opposite direction. "We passed a lofty promontory in the latitude of 59 degrees 10 minutes and the longitude of 207 degrees 45 minutes," Cook wrote. "As the discovery of it was with the Princess Elizabeth's birth day I named it Cape Elizabeth."

Captain Cook was searching for a Northwest Passage. The continents—Eurasia and Africa, North and South America— were arranged so inconveniently. Stretched out from the ice-bound north to the stormy south, the shape of the land was a formidable obstacle to trade. Europeans wanted a shortcut to Asia. But over the previous few centuries, expeditions along the northern coast of Russia—in the Northeast Passage—had failed in the ice. West was the only way left. Cartographers penned hopeful, navigable channels, carved through the sprawling mystery of North America. Real men looked for them. Cook arrived at the helm of the HMS *Resolution* with specific instructions: "to proceed northward along the coast, as far as the latitude of 65 degrees or farther, if you are not obstructed by lands or ice, taking care not to lose any time in exploring rivers or inlets, or upon any other account." He also carried instructions to claim land for the British Crown, but it seemed like more an afterthought. Alaska was an obstacle, not a prize.

CANADA

ALASKA

Knik Arm

Susitna
Delta

Beluga

Anchorage

Girdwood

Tyonek

*Chickaloon
Bay*

*Trading
Bay*

Point
Possession

Hope

Turnagain Arm

Kustatan
Peninsula

Nikiski

Drift River

Kenai River

Kenai

Soldotna

Kasilof River

Crescent River

Chisik Island

Kenai Peninsula

Silver Salmon
Creek Lodge

Ninilchik

Iniskin
Peninsula

COOK INLET

Anchor
Point

Kachemak Selo

Homer

*Aurora
Lagoon*

Ursus Head

Kachemak Bay

Bruin Bay

Seldovia

*Kamishak
Bay*

Nanwalek

McNeil
River
Camp

Dogfish Bay
START: March 27

Cape Douglas

Mount
Douglas

Four-Peaked Lake
END: July 12

Sukoi Bay

∿ Our route

◆ Inhabited places

○ Points of interest

N
↑

50 miles

The entrance to Cook Inlet is only a little north of 59 degrees latitude. The bulk of the Alaska coast bends south here, but the inlet turns north. Cook might have missed sailing into it at all, but on the morning his ships sailed by, fog obscured the western shore, turning the mountains into a series of disconnected peaks that appeared as a range of volcanic islands. Cook knew that the Alaska of Russian maps had been drawn as an island, which meant that somewhere—here!—a passage separated it from the mass of North America. Full of hope that he had found the Northwest Passage at last, he turned north.

To me, the strangest thing is that Cook actually expected to find a Northwest Passage. That anyone believed it was likely that a great ocean passage would cut through a continent—in a stunning display of geography-for-human-convenience unparalleled by anything in the mapped world. But that's an explorer for you: optimistic confidence in the improbable and a drive to learn on the ground, even when it may seem difficult or futile.

Perhaps my family shared Cook's pigheadedness. For my husband, Hig, and me, tossing aside all the dishes and sweeping away computers and phones for the wild open shores of Cook Inlet was an addictive thrill. The maps we carried showed every nook and cranny of the inlet's coastline. They showed them flat, four-colored (ocean, forest, alpine, ice), meticulously surveyed, and with just enough detail to leave me hopelessly curious. We were tracing the maps in search of what they couldn't possibly show—the feel of Cook Inlet's mud in our eyebrows, the taste of its plump razor clams, the sound of its crying seal pups and humming oil rigs, and the stories of its fishermen and teachers. We were tracing the maps to find out what was really out there right now and what might be out there in the future. There was so much to learn, so much to explore.

Captain Cook had labeled the inlet as a river. Although he left its name blank, the inlet that would later bear his name is more than two hundred miles long and more than fifty miles wide at the mouth. Its eastern shore holds around 350,000 of

Alaska's 730,000 people, clumped into the city of Anchorage, strung out along the highway to Homer, and dotted into the few villages beyond the end of the road. Fat brown bears lumber along the wild western shore, outnumbering the handful of fish camps, oil camps, Native villagers, and camera-toting tourists. The inlet's mouth is crinkled with toothy fjords and melting glaciers. Its head is a sweep of quicksand mud. Its waters swirl with thick brown silt and roiling tidal currents, teeming salmon and endangered belugas, fishing boats and oil rigs and otters. Perhaps you shouldn't listen to the biases of a resident, but Cook Inlet's got it all—all the wild and human drama—all the glaciers and the bears and the things I cherish most about this state I've chosen. It is the heart of Alaska.

Hig and I didn't know of anyone who had walked and paddled around the entire shore of Cook Inlet. Alaska is rich in places that almost no one ever walks. It's a good place for an explorer, an easy place to be awed by, to be curious about, to draw a bold line across the map and claim a journey of your own. It would be harder, of course, to actually do it beneath the crushing weight of Lituya, our two-year-old, and with as much lightweight titanium and nylon as a family of four must carry. As for our four-year-old, Katmai, there is a dearth of information on explorers of his age. All I knew is that he was much too big to be carried on an eight-hundred-mile expedition. He was incredibly excited at the prospect of doing the journey on his own two feet. *We're going around Cook Inlet!*

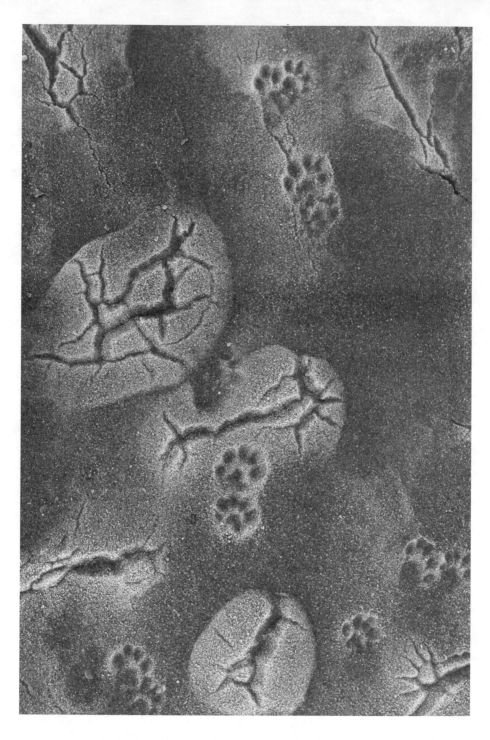

River otter tracks in the frozen sand, on a small beach between the rocky cliffs of outer Cook Inlet.

HUMAN SCALE

MARCH 27–30: DOGFISH BAY TO NANWALEK

The sky was a small dark square in a streaky window above the fishing boat's sink. I fixed on it with a stubborn gaze, trying not to puke again. I stumbled to the heavy door, scooted myself out onto the deck, and shivered in the blast that crinkled my nose hairs and slicked the rails with salt ice. We'd left at four a.m. with the tide, and a few hours later it was still completely dark. I stared at the horizon—wasn't that supposed to help with motion sickness?—and watched the moon shimmering sickly yellow on the waves.

Finally the motor stopped. Clutching the arm of a toddler in each mittened hand, I shuffle-skated to the railing and peered down through the icy bars. I left the kids to climb over the fishing boat's edge and plunged into our packraft. The buckle that was supposed to clip my overstuffed backpack to my packraft was broken. My mitten was starting to ice over from where I'd accidentally dipped it in the sea. The crowd of fishermen on deck was staring, and I fumbled, painfully aware of the schedule the crew was trying to keep. Hig passed the kids, Lituya and Katmai—each a puffball of snow gear in a life vest—over the fishing boat's railing. Now settled in the packraft, I balanced them on my lap. Hig scrambled into his own boat. We shoved off.

My family bobbed in the waves. The fishing boat lit up the sea as it motored off in search of cod. Eight hundred miles between us and the end of our journey.

Where does an inlet start? We'd chosen Dogfish Bay as the official beginning of our journey around Cook Inlet. In a line drawn end to end on a Google Earth map, this bay seemed to roughly delineate the mouth of the inlet. It was as good as any nearby bay or cove. And the fishing boat ride had been free.

Modern expeditions are always a bit contrived. Our stories hang within a framework of self-selected rules, like the syllables in a haiku. Two little-known dents in the coast—Dogfish Bay on the east and Sukoi Bay on the west—would serve as endpoints for this particular grand scheme. Over the next three to four months, we planned to use a few pairs of shoes and a couple of five-foot-long packrafts to trace the shoreline of Cook Inlet, by human power, with our children, ages four and two. It was late March, still more winter than spring, but it would be spring-brown soon, we hoped, and summer-green before we returned. I'd spent years watching the sun set on a skyline of volcanoes, orange light streaking across Cook Inlet and into the windows of my home, twenty-six miles up the coast in the village of Seldovia. So why not walk there? Why not walk even farther? Why not begin at the tip of the Kenai Peninsula and end at Cape Douglas? Why not swallow the entire glorious outline of Alaska's Cook Inlet?

It was, of course, an outlandish plan. Anyone in their right mind might have pointed out the bears, the tidal currents, the quicksand, or the storms. Or that eight hundred miles is actually quite far, and two-year-olds are actually quite heavy. Or that four-year-olds are not known for their straight-line hiking speed and that humans invented motorized transportation for a good reason. But no one bothered to point it out. Our friends knew us too well. For Hig and me, an eight-hundred-mile, human-powered trip with the kids is nothing out of the ordinary. For more than a decade, we've made a habit of these expeditions. It's what everyone expects of us.

We take big trips every other year. It sounds so commonplace scheduled out like that. No different than "I spend winters in Hawaii." And it isn't all that different. Until we find ourselves immersed in spreadsheets listing gear and the phone numbers of distant friends of friends who might be able to bring a box of food to a remote inlet in the middle of June. Staring at weather data for April, wondering how many layers might keep a two-year-old warm. Debating just how far a four-year-old can hike in a day. Counting miles on the map and guessing where we'll be when the bears wake up. Until we paddle onto the shore at dawn, surrounded by the fruits of our months of planning in one giant misshapen backpack.

We landed on the beach at Dogfish Bay, scraping the packrafts against the gravel. Salt ice slicked the edges of the boats, shattering into white chips as Hig rolled them up. Katmai ran circles around us in his impatience. "We're going around Cook Inlet! We're going around Cook Inlet!" His life vest was still clipped over his shiny blue jacket, and the edge of a flowery fleece hood hung lopsided over one eye. Lituya sat on the beach, rubbing her eyes with mittened hands. "I want to go back to the van!" Her freckled nose crinkled into a pout, framed by several layers of hats and hoods and a wisp of tousled red hair. If she rode in a van to leave her house in the wee hours of the morning, surely she should be able to get back in and drive home.

"No, Lituya. Grandma's van is very far away. Our home is a tent home now."

The graying light revealed a gravel beach striped with tide lines of kelp. Ice falls curtained the cliffs at the top of the beach, and the hills above them rose steeply into dark spruce and white snow. It could just as well have been our beach at home. A couple hours as the fishing boat growls, maybe a week or so for us, until we could say hi to Grandma in Seldovia and keep right on walking. We were explorers of the already mapped, of the close-at-hand, discovering this land more than six thousand years after its first explorers.

A few hours later, Katmai's fevered excitement and his sister's confusion had tumbled into slumber. We were paddling again, one sleeping kid on each parental lap. I adjusted Lituya's hood to block the wind from her face. Salt ice formed a brittle frosting on every boulder and sea spire, reaching fifty feet above our heads, up into the twisted trees and ragged winter grass. Above that, clusters of fuzzy white dots—mountain goats—grazed on the slopes.

"It's getting kind of choppy out here," I noted.

"Yeah, I think the next point will be too exposed," Hig agreed.

"Not sure there's anywhere to land right here, though."

"I'm sure there's somewhere." Hig, ever the optimist.

"Then what?" I was always the realist, the planner. We debated our options. Landings were rare among the cliffs. Flat campsites, probably rarer. Maybe we could walk the coast at a lower tide but not now. And what if the weather worsened? No decision, even on the very first day, would be simple.

We were going around Cook Inlet. But first, we were going around Point Adam, an insignificant little finger of coastline where icy spires plunged into the waves. We couldn't see the end—couldn't see the far shore any more than Captain Cook had. The inlet was a blur of gray, stretching into the misty distance. Our planning for a hundred days and several hundred miles was a blur of numbers, also stretching into the misty distance. My lists of logistics had jumped from town to town, resupply spot to resupply spot, as if we might simply step from one to another: Nanwalek, Port Graham, Seldovia, China Poot,

Vosnesenska, Homer, Williamsport, McNeil River, Sukoi Bay. Which things go in which box? Who do we talk to in this town or that? Where do we send the bear fence, the summer tent? How much food from town A to town B, and how big should the fudge factor be? To fully prepare, I had to grasp hold of that whole eight hundred miles.

Here on the first day, all of that fell away. After traveling less than one one-hundredth of the distance, the inlet seemed so vast—the trip suddenly so much bigger than I'd imagined. At the same time, it seemed so small, so simple. It was nothing more than the rocky shore above us and deciding where to camp. It was as relaxing as it was intimidating. We had returned to human scale.

Hig and I scoured the icy forest, wrenching on every visible stick for something unfrozen enough to lift, yet heavy enough to help anchor the tent. "Why do we never do anything easy?" Hig asked, trying to drive wooden stakes into the concrete-like duff. I squatted, yanking on a firmly stuck log. Through the screen of branches, we could see the foaming white breaks below us. We had abandoned the increasingly choppy water hours ago, found a landing, and managed to scramble up a bit of dirt between the cliffs to reach the forest, where a steep and icy traverse was made extra slippery by a powder dusting of snow. We had back-tracked to this flat spot. The traverse wasn't worth it. This ice floor was as good as we'd get.

The kids answered their father's question with an impatient whine. Their day, like ours, had started long before dawn. I shrugged, and gave Hig our standard answer: "Because that's how you have an adventure." Inside the tent, we sawed branches and fed them into the small titanium wood stove we carried. Outside the tent, the nearly full moon rose behind a screen of clouds that warmed the night to just below freezing. We slept as the moon and sun tugged the water, combining to bring us the extreme tides that made these dramatic shores even more dramatic.

The next morning, the ocean drew back, leaving a path below the cliffs. We walked on sculpted terraces of rock, decorated with a seaweed fringe. The swath of slippery seaweed and barnacles hissed and crackled in the air. There was a sense of abundance in those thick fronds of kelp, hiding glints of color that were blood-red sea stars or fuzzy orange sponges. Sparrows flitted from rock to rock, flicking their tails. Katmai sprinted down the beach, then stopped to watch a snail crawling across the palm of my hand. Lituya stood on the rocks, cheering for the water to hit, daring it to splash her, then laughing and shrieking at the bubbles as they lapped at the toes of her boots.

Sometimes it was like that. Other times, it was translucent sheets of sleet, blowing sideways into trees that had grown into twisted pretzels from years of such assaults, as we picked our way around the spiny stalks of devil's club that bristled from the forest floor. Or it was holding the hand of a reluctant child, hurrying around a point before the tide covered the only walkable path. Riding spruce-branch horsies for hours, and more hours, waiting for the water to retreat. The tides drew in and out in a rhythm that controlled us. They uncovered and re-covered our walking paths, while the wind-whipped ocean kept us off of the water. They revealed an abundance of life that made me want to peer under every rock. But I couldn't. Take a minute to look, then hurry on. You can't always paddle, and you can't always walk, so you'd better take advantage of the low tide while you have it. Just try and explain that to a four-year-old.

Hig and I had done lots of things like this before. Thousands of miles of expeditions crisscrossing Alaska's edges. But each journey had been under the power of our own grown-up legs. Now, for the first time, our son was not just part of the load we carried. He was a full-fledged member of the team. Every mile we walked would have to be walked with the willing participation of someone who couldn't yet tie his own shoes. The four months we'd allocated for this expedition was a wild guess. With Katmai on foot, would it be seven months? Would he lie down somewhere along the way and refuse to go farther? This was only the first leg of the journey. These four days passed by at an average of three and a half slow, difficult miles each day. I didn't need a calculator to make me feel like one of the snails we walked beside.

Adventures are supposed to be a rite of passage. Someone naive, usually young, maybe in midlife crisis, has an existential break with their ordinary life and sets out into the sleet-whipped mountains to find themselves. At which point they say, "Hey, self! How about we go in and have a coffee somewhere a little more comfortable?" And they do. For some of us, it works differently. I yell, "Hey, self!" and the self says, "Isn't it beautiful the way the sleet builds up on the edges of the cliff? I wonder why this forest is different than the one in the last fjord? Do you think we can make it through that pass?" And then she's gone, me chasing behind.

More than a decade ago, I was seeking to find myself, and I found an explorer, a self twisted with an insatiable curiosity about everything and everyone. I found a like-minded husband along the way, and we had kids just like us, because all kids are curious like that. Adventuring is our unpaid, slush-in-your-shoes, hungry, grubby, transformative family business. Somehow, we've managed to build a life that revolves around traveling incredible distances, incredibly slowly. It seems like we get slower every year. We're no Native paddlers, and no Captain Cook. But we *are* a family of explorers.

We washed up in Nanwalek village like the survivors from a shipwrecked vessel. A man on a four-wheeler came down to check on us before we'd even taken off our life vests—making sure that the family in little rubber rafts was doing this intentionally. We said our awkward hellos, rolled up the packrafts under the dozens of eyes peering out of windows, and walked the path into town, wondering what rumors were preceding us.

A plume of smoke curls from the wood stove in our tent while we are camped on an icy beach.

GOING
VISITING

I'd never visited the villages of Nanwalek or Port Graham, but our box of food had done so several times already. Tossed into the back of a Cessna for the ten-mile flight, it had been summarily rejected by the Nanwalek Post Office—when you know all two hundred residents, a strange name clearly indicates a wrong address—and sent back to the Cessna to repeat the loop, until the fed-up air taxi finally called us just before we set out: "Can you just let us know when you get there, and we'll put it on the next plane?"

Hig had run down to meet the plane, while the kids and I waited in the arctic entry of the little grocery store, next to the tacked-up community announcements. The store looked like most village stores: Costco packages broken apart for individual sale; aisles of rice and diapers and soda with alarmingly high prices; freezers of meat and a handful of fresh items. The crackers and candy were exactly what we already had, so I bought the kids bananas and tomatoes for a treat, while I snacked on a $7 paper cup of pickled local bidarki (a.k.a. Black Katy chiton). The orange flesh of this palm-sized marine invertebrate—a headless black slug with a line of knobby white plates—is only slightly less tough than its shells. But pickling had transformed it into something tasty I'd appreciate even if I hadn't been living on dried camping food with a few fronds of boiled seaweed. The only people we'd seen since we left the fishing boat four days ago were bidarki hunters—a family roaming the fjords with skiff and buckets, enjoying one of the few calm afternoons.

Bidarki—meaning "little kayak"—is a Russian word. Captain Cook left this inlet within two weeks of his arrival, but right here, in 1785, the Russians built their first settlement on the North American mainland. This was Fort Alexandrovsk, or Alexander Redoubt. They had chopped trees to erect a twelve-foot palisade, where twenty buildings squatted inside a guarded square, 120 yards on each side. A handful of Russian men, in search of ruthless profit, lived briefly and uneasily at this uncomfortable outpost, beneath Russia's imperial coat of arms. They were *promyshlenniki*. Siberian contract workers. Fur trappers. Rugged wilderness dwellers who pushed ever eastward across Siberia and hopped islands into Alaska, where they beached their ships for the winter, lived in driftwood huts and Aleut clothes, ate the meat and fish and blubber that the Aleuts did, and made the Aleuts do their hunting for them. Promyshlenniki were skilled hunters on land, but not on the sea.

The sea held the wealth of Alaska. While Captain Cook was seeking a way around America, the Russians wanted America itself. Compared to the harsh landscape of Siberia, the coastline of North America seemed lush, rich, promising. Tsar Peter I the Great (and later Empress Anna) sent Danish explorer Vitus Bering in 1724 and again in 1741 to sail beyond the edge of Russia's eastern fringe. First to see if Alaska was connected to Russia, and next to explore Alaska itself. The Russians imagined gold and silver to rival the Spanish colonies, but any wealth would do. The sea otter furs that Bering's shipmates brought back were an accidental by-product of a winter spent starving and hunting on an uninhabited island.

From then on, the promyshlenniki, and the investors who backed them, wanted nothing more than those otter furs that had fetched such a handsome price in China. The promyshlenniki had so thoroughly decimated the Siberian sable that they'd been importing furs from London to resell. They typically wouldn't have bothered building a fort. The promyshlenniki scraped by as needed. But this time their boss, Grigorii Shelikov, had more colonial ambitions. He shipped in seeds and cattle, built a school for local boys, and set about creating Alaska's first "European" town on Kodiak Island. Shelikov sent his men to Nanwalek in 1785 to build this more distant outpost—the first European settlement on the North American mainland.

Russians occupied Alaska for around a hundred years—from the first hunting camps on the Aleutians in the mid-1700s to the sale of Alaska to the United States in 1867. Along the way, they killed many of those who had occupied it first. Just off of Kodiak Island, Shelikov led his promyshlenniki in a massacre at Refuge Rock, in which hundreds, maybe even thousands, of Natives were bombarded by Russian cannons on a tiny island where they had fled for refuge. Such force was illegal under Russian law, but the law was difficult to enforce on this far-flung frontier. The Russians killed in quieter ways too. They forced men to hunt otters and women to provide them with food and clothing. Hunters from the Aleutians were sent on voyages of thousands of miles. Sometimes villagers starved for the want of the food they'd have otherwise been hunting for themselves. Disease was a scourge here, as it was in all of the colonial world. Of the Native groups in closest contact with the Russians, maybe 80 percent of the population was lost during Russian occupation.

The Russians also mimicked the Natives they lived with. Depended on them. Although the promyshlenniki signed up for five-year contracts, they often had to wait many years for a ship from home. Supplying the new colony from Russia proved nearly impossible. The only clothes were Native clothes. The only food was Native food, and it was the Natives themselves who obtained it. "Foxes and ground squirrels," noted one visiting observer, "were the only animals that the Russians were capable of killing." Marriages among the Russians to Native women were encouraged. According to a letter to Shelikov's successor who would manage the Kodiak colony, Shelikov provided for their wedding gifts: "Make an effort to see to it that the single settlers being sent [to Alaska] presently marry fine upstanding American girls; to this end I have sent you various items, necessary complements to clothing, as gifts for the brides and future wives; at weddings, supply each groom with same."

Families were built from these marriages. In all the years of Russian occupation, there were never more than eight hundred Russians in Alaska at a time. But by 1839, a Russian Orthodox priest counted nearly thirteen hundred half-Russian half-Native children. Egg-domed churches popped up along the coast. Local languages were written with Cyrillic characters, recorded in a partnership with Russian Orthodox priests. These same priests delivered smallpox vaccines to their converts. Last names like Kvasnikoff and Lestenkoff were left behind, as well as the traces of Russian bloodlines, the Russian Orthodox church and its icons (which still grace the walls of modern Nanwalek homes), and the language of local foods and everyday objects.

One of the few remaining speakers of the Sugpiat language (only thirty people speak it today) in Nanwalek pointed out to me: "A lot of our newer words—like 'table' and 'chair'—come from Russian. We didn't have those things before." Her name was Pauline, and with her husband, Jerry, we talked history around a wooden table, while a flock of grandchildren—just a few of their forty—flitted in and out. Protective older girls drew Lituya outside to play in the patchy snow. Katmai sat next to me, his legs dangling off the chair, eating our hosts' crackers and launching into a history of the prehistoric animals he was obsessed with.

We only had a day in Nanwalek, which was as much as we expected to have in most walled-in structures, with all the time it takes us to get from one to the next. But we wanted to visit them all—every village, city, fish camp, and outpost we could reach on the shores of Cook Inlet. Packed in my waterproof pouch, with all the bits and pieces of gear that became useful only in the presence of civilization—driver's license, credit card, a black plastic comb—I carried a question. Each time we cornered an unsuspecting soul, I unpacked it: "What do you think this place—Alaska, Cook Inlet, this town—will be like in fifty years? A hundred? What does the future hold?"

"I don't know," said Jerry, passing Katmai another packet of crackers, before resting his arms on the shiny table. Which is what I would have said too, if someone had asked me this question out of the blue. Jerry probably didn't know what he was in for, when he'd talked to us on the phone and agreed to meet at the house with the rhino four-wheelers out front. Jerry and Pauline, both with long gray hair and in rounded glasses, looked the contented part of grandparents. A TV and half a dozen small voices chattered in the next room. Katmai ran out of prehistoric creatures to discuss, popped the last cracker in his mouth, and ended his monologue with "What *other* snacks do you have?" Some of the grandchildren ran by for drawing supplies. We talked about the future. Jerry wanted his grandkids in fiber-optic engineering and the kind of high-tech jobs that don't, and may never, exist in the village. But he loved having his family close by.

As teacher of a language that so few people speak, Pauline held a version of the future that sounded more like a lament. "The younger people know some of the words, but the ability to have a conversation is lost. Sugpiat, it sounds like the birds, coming from deep in the throat, or through the nose. . . . And a lot of them can't pronounce it." Pauline and Jerry told me about an elder who was reviving the tradition of building skin-covered kayaks. Yet only the white teachers, they said, go kayaking.

Skiffs are faster. This is the first time in thousands of years that kayaks aren't practical. The couple of dozen men whom Shelikov stationed at Fort Alexandrovsk were 150 miles from their main outpost on Kodiak and many thousands of miles from their Russian roots. Perhaps they only saw their other country-men in the annual flotilla of hunting bidarkas as they proceeded from Kodiak to Prince William Sound and beyond, decimating sea otters along the way. Wooden sailing ships carried treasures and the news of distant nations, but most of the work was done by the paddlers.

Nanwalek, and the neighboring village of Port Graham, were both behind us. I paused, letting the sun spark against the drips of water on my paddle blades, watching each one plop into the jagged red reflection of the raft. My raft, which has the approximate tracking capability of the kids' bathtime toys, spun lazy circles in the middle of Port Graham Bay. A packraft is no bidarka. Even when I paddle, the bow wiggles back and forth with every stroke, swinging across an average of mostly straight. My son's boots pressed into my calves where he knelt on my legs, leaning over the pack strapped to the front of my raft, staring at the shore beyond. Our view slowly panned from a small, forest-tufted island to the village behind us. An oil rig anchored beside the little dock stretched to the sky and dwarfed the buildings behind it, like the masts of the Russian sailing ships once did. Then we spun farther, looking out to an expanse of open blue and the white peaks beyond.

We were half an hour beyond Port Graham and a few days beyond Nanwalek, a week or so into our journey. The fog had dissolved into cold spring sun. And while Captain Cook had been devastated to see the inlet's narrowing shores rise up around him, Hig and I greeted the first clear day with enthusiasm. Our destination was revealed. Cape Douglas was a wide mess of triangular lumps—snow white, haze blue—a smudge in the squinting distance. It squatted across fifty-five miles of ocean, marking our end point on the far side of Cook Inlet's mouth. Impossibly more distant given our actual pace and route.

I wasn't nearly as bold as those bidarka paddlers had been. They just crossed that vast opening. First for their own reasons, later for the Russians—hundreds of tiny little boats that were sometimes dozens of miles from any shore. I wondered how they judged the weather. What conditions would they travel in? How fast? How slow? What were they scared of? What would it be like to carry those generations of knowledge and skill in place of the map zipped into my coat pocket?

"Katmai, do you see those mountains out there?" I pointed across the fifty-five miles of blue. "That's where we're going!"

"But I want to go to *shore!*"

"Oh," I explained. "I mean, those mountains are where we're going when we get all the way done with going around Cook Inlet. In the summer. Not where we're going right *now*. We will go to shore, right over there somewhere." I nodded in a general northward direction. "As soon as your sister is done with her nap." But where *were* we going?

Our final destination of Cape Douglas was mostly arbitrary, ridiculously far (at the pace of a wiggling packraft and a walking four-year-old), and rather theoretical, even from an adult point of view. We were also headed to Anchorage, about 150 miles northwest as the helicopter flies, where a red and black Lifeline helicopter had lifted off to this morning, taking a patient who had waited through the night. This village is remote still. No roads reach it, and village health aides fill the gap between here and a big city hospital. But not so remote as to require a months-long journey. No one has to travel as slowly as we are, not anymore.

I picked up my paddle again, hurrying to put this minor crossing of Port Graham Bay behind us. Not because of my son's insistent whines that he had to get to shore *right now*, or because my husband was already a few hundred yards ahead with my sleeping daughter, or even because I had to pee. This clear calm, cold sun, glassy water—it felt as tense as a held breath. I needed to get around the point before the world exhaled again.

The sky held its breath, across Port Graham Bay, at Coal Cove, around Dangerous Cape—which seemed, as we drifted in a raft of sleeping sea otters, inaptly named. A baby otter awakened from its nap with a human-sounding scream. Both baby and mother flipped onto their bellies, contorting to keep their dry paws above water as they wiggled away from us. Other sea otters bobbed in the kelp, unconcerned. I dug out my sunglasses, as Hig smeared sunblock on Lituya's freckled nose and gleaming pale cheekbones. We eventually landed on the beach. The day felt slow, relaxed, like the kind of fun that anyone would recognize. I watched the kids recede into smaller spots as they ran ahead on sand and cobbles, letting them go because the cold, the storms, and even the bears were still asleep.

A straight line drawn from Port Graham to our next stop at Seldovia is only seven and a half miles. But I've tried pieces of that straight line—crawling past steep cliffs, spiny devil's club, and alder so twisted you wonder if you ought to have practiced your yoga before entering. Along the shore, the beaches are punctuated by knobby cliffs that can be skirted only at extreme low tide. Some can't be skirted at all. You might not have a sailing ship, or a skiff, or ferry, or a bidarka, or even a modern plastic kayak, but you have to have something that floats.

Packrafts float. Brightly colored, tough-coated high-tech polyurethane, they look like pool toys. But these five-pound, five-foot wonders can shoot a thrill-seeker over a boiling waterfall or carry a hunter's just-killed moose. Deflated, we could shove two of them into Hig's overstuffed pack. They pop up all over Alaska and, increasingly, all over the world. Yet people rarely bring them into the ocean. Perhaps it's the psychological vulnerability of the enterprise, paddling out to sea with only a pillow of air between you and the big blue water. They're slow and tiny, and if you leave a packraft untethered on a windy day, it might even blow away. We carry them because they're the only boats you could possibly carry for hundreds of miles. We love them because they're sturdy—barnacle-scraping, wave-riding sturdy. We curse them in every encounter with the surf.

The crux of things, on an expedition, is often so small. A twenty-foot cliff, a thirty-foot river, or a fifty-foot band of breakers between sand and glassy sea. We were packrafters—joyfully amphibious travelers spending long hours meandering along the beaches and equally long hours poking our rafts' rubber noses into gurgling sea caves. The kids could clamber over boulders and then sleep off their wild antics on our laps, heads tucked beneath the spin of the paddle shaft. I could stretch my cramped legs with long strides across the sand, then relieve my sore shoulders by letting the water carry us all. I could run my fingers over the rough ribs of a cockle fossilized in sand, then dip my paddle blades between fronds of kelp. Two awesome worlds; one heck of a job to cross between them.

We were launching. Katmai perched on the top of a seaweed-slick boulder, stuffed into a life vest over all his winter clothes. Hig stood on another boulder, Lituya clutched in his arms. The field of slippery boulders was supposed to make our job easier. Water sloshed between gaps in the rocks, which cut the break of the swell, sending small waves jumping in every direction. It wasn't a windy day. This was the best March had to offer, here on Cook Inlet's exposed outer edge.

I watched as a wave splashed over the toes of my boots, then I jumped in the raft, water streaming from my feet. I whirled my arms like a broken ceiling fan, choppy and fast and not very rhythmic, as I dodged the boulders that broke the waves, shooting between the small breakers into the calm water beyond. I turned, settled down into the raft seat, and watched the waves roll past, waiting for a smaller set.

The kids looked a little shocked at being forgotten on shore. I turned back, rushing in on the back of a smaller set of waves, a bumper car bouncing off the rock where Hig stood, holding up a life-vested toddler like an offering to the wave gods. The water drew down around me and the raft bent backward. I was beached, for a moment, on a conical rock. Hig set Lituya into my boat, then gave me a shove as the water surged forward again, and I windmilled out beyond the waves. Katmai whined from his perch. I couldn't understand him, but I yelled that he was next, and Hig grabbed him for the pass off.

Small swells rolled beneath me, not quite breaking, as I dashed back to repeat the procedure, plucking Katmai from Hig's arms to set him almost on top of Lituya, taking a half wave over the side of the raft. Even that was cold. The whole thing was awkward and stressful. Hig filmed it all on a camera strapped to his head. The kids whined in concert, shoving each other aside in a failure to share space—three people in a single tiny raft. I whined too. I bribed them with candy. Then there was chocolate and, finally, calm.

There were more sea otters, and the blinding stripe of sun bounced off ocean. According to Katmai, there were even Plesiosaurs, their immense swanlike necks popping up among the kelp. It took an hour of agonizing over just which boulder to launch from and only a few minutes to muddle through it, and if I shifted my butt above the pool that half-wave had sloshed in, I could forget it entirely. The crux of things, on an expedition, is often so small.

I opened a bag of pretzel crumbs, and we turned our paddles across Seldovia Bay—toward home. It wasn't an accident that we'd grown fascinated by the water that laps our own shores. We wanted to trace the outline of Cook Inlet, and our own village—Seldovia—was on it. It was neither the start nor the end of the journey. Neither the most important landmark nor the least. Just stop number three in the couple dozen we had planned.

When we got to Seldovia, we didn't even go home. Only a short road of memorized curves connected the beach we landed on to the yurt we lived in, but that home was cold and empty and a few miles uphill in the wrong direction. Today, home was our tent on a snowy beach. Did it really matter how many times we'd come here for potlucks and low tides and kid hikes and bonfires? It was as familiar as the skyline of volcanoes on the other side of the inlet. We were going there too, traveling into our own million-dollar view.

On the beach, my kids' friends crawled in and out of the tent, fascinated by the tiny wood stove and the fortlike nature of our current residence. Adults stood around the campfire, in the strip of gravel between tide and snow, eating potluck food from paper plates, talking about much the same things we always do: houses being built, the latest and future travel plans, pregnancies, and the weather forecast. We talked about where we could put a rope tow to take the kids skiing. Is it worth it to chip a broken tractor out of the ice and send the engine to Anchorage for fixing? What's it like in the villages? Our friends asked how the trip was going. And then: "Are you having fun?"

"Oh, yeah, everything's going great so far. The weather was pretty harsh when we started, but it's been beautiful the last few days." Then I didn't know what to say. An expedition is about as fun as parenthood. Or life. Trips *include* fun, but they are bigger than fun—every aspect of the adventure blends into something greater than the sum of its parts. One bald eagle flapping over the ocean with a squid dangling from its talons, plus one frigid sleet storm, plus two cozy evenings chatting with newly made friends, plus several surf launches, plus three pots of popcorn eaten over campfires, plus uncountable tantrums and diaper changes, plus uncountable otters and playful conversations. . . . How do you solve that equation? The negatives and positives fail to cancel each other out. They grow into a story.

The next morning I took another step down an icy trail, stopped, and looked behind me again, my face betraying a rising impatience. Lituya was following, inching step after inching step after squatting down to examine the pattern of crystals on a frozen-over puddle. "You know," Hig commented, "it seems funny to choose the slowest mode of transportation in the world, then try to hurry up. With kids, it's even more so."

I laughed in spite of myself. "A walking two-year-old *is* the slowest thing in the world." So we hurried the slowest hurry in the world, from a friend's house, to another friend's wall tent, to the beach, paddling off to be tremendously late to meet some other friends.

We chatted, then walked, then blew up the rafts, then paddled out of sight of the last of the Seldovia houses. We were going where we always go—on every expedition we've ever undertaken. We were leaving our home beach behind for shores we'd never walked, people we'd never met, and weather we couldn't predict. We were headed to a building, which contained a box, which contained noodles and butter and chocolate and potato chips. We were going to the next dot on the map, and the next name on the list of logistics held in my waterproof notebook. The stop through home made it feel like we'd finished an adventure and started a whole new one, with barely a breath in between. But adventures are just another sort of home. We slipped back into the well-planned unknown.

The kids play in the cabin of a shipwrecked boat, where we cooked a meal out of the wind.

PLEISTOCENE DAYS

APRIL 6-10: SELDOVIA TO AURORA LAGOON

"Your mittens!" Katmai shrieked, chasing them across the sand. I'd set them down to adjust a strap. Katmai dove and then stood up triumphantly, my two yellow mittens clutched in his two blue ones. I tugged them back over my ragged gloves, then pinched the string Hig passed over my shoulder. He was weaving my torso in a web of slipknots, strapping a pair of partially inflated sleeping pads to the long underwear, puffy coat, rain coat, and toddler I was already wearing.

The wind was at our backs. It bit through Lituya's hood and chewed at her ankles where the snow pants rode up above the tops of her woolly socks. It was naptime and the wind rushed up Kachemak Bay, jerking the sleeping pad out of Hig's hand as he fought to secure it. The slick white Spectra cord was probably strong enough to climb on. Hig's knots, well-practiced and largely infallible, were tucked behind my back. I'd better not need out of this without help. The unsecured edge of a sleeping pad flapped in the wind—gray, yellow, gray, yellow, gray, yellow. Lituya whimpered, wiggling her face into my neck.

I stretched my arm down to Katmai again, grasping his hand in my own. Half his words were blocked by the balaclava covering his mouth. The other half were drowned out by the wind. Hand in hand, mitten in mitten, we walked down the long sand spit toward China Poot Bay—Katmai's incessant and unintelligible chatter, the limp silence of Lituya asleep on my back, the crash of surf, and the shriek of the wind.

There was no room, in my puffed-up costume, for a water bottle. I left it in the fanny pack, ice creeping in from all the edges, just a few brackish gulps in the column in the middle. Those were for the kids, anyway. Seagulls flew spirals in the curling surf, their white wings flashing against the turquoise and white of the water we'd never dare paddle in. It didn't matter. As much as I depended on—even loved—those rafts curled up in Hig's backpack, I liked walking the beach even more.

Everything comes to the beach. Earlier that morning, we'd woken to find the glistening six-foot body of a sleeper shark washed up a few yards from the tent. Only its eye had been pecked out by the birds, and the sand was still swept into small piles from the struggle of tail and fins. A trail of vomit dribbled from its toothy mouth. It wasn't yet frozen. It hadn't expected to be somewhere so shallow. We all crouched around a second washed-up shark—the kids' faces fascinated, the shark's face jagged and pink around another pecked-out eye. This shark was sliced and tracked by the ravens, now freezing as solid as the driftwood logs. If the bears were awake, they'd be walking this tide line with us.

The rivers come down to the beach as well, spitting out stones and fallen trees and the gritty brown swirls of mountains chewed by ice. At least that's what they usually do. Last night I'd wandered for thirty minutes through the toe-deep channels of a broad glacial river before plunging all our bottles into the least brackish pool. I scurried back to the tent to rewarm my wet hands—painfully—by our tiny wood stove. I was surprised. This was the river that everyone rafts in summertime. We should have known better, should have realized that the water wouldn't return until the world thawed and the glacier melted, that any remaining trickle could disappear between the rocks. The unspoken words hung over the frosted stones: "Why didn't you guys wait until summer?"

So I could wade the whole river without going over the tops of my boots? Of course there are logistics—bear seasons and tourist seasons and gardening seasons—and perhaps a dollop of unfounded optimism about conditions unknown and unseen. But the world is a different place when most people don't see it; the ocean empty of the whine of skiffs, the glow of gold rye grass against white-draped mountains; the state park trails marked with a single line of ski tracks and the steps of coyotes.

The next thing the beach brought us was the front of a boat. It was silvered wood and empty windows, painted with yellow rosettes of lichen and the brownish tufts of winter moss. The cabin that once hid its captain from sea spray now hid two children from the wind, giggling and wrestling in the tiny fort made by the fo'c'sle. "Do you think we could get our stovepipe through the hole in the roof?" I asked the kids. We could. Hig and I cooked popcorn and mashed potatoes in the fort, with almost the last of the water, while the kids played and the wind flattened the grass and rattled the nylon of my raincoat, and the tide dropped, flattening the waves.

We'd reached the spot where spit meets fjord, and there was nothing left but to paddle. At three miles long and less than half a mile wide, China Poot Bay is a smallish fjord, just a dimple on Kachemak Bay's jagged southern shore. This coast is carved in fjords; ancient rock smeared onto the edge of the continent by the movement of the plates, cut with the incisions of ice age glaciers. They crumple the coastline from Washington State to the Aleutian chain. They are the teeth in Cook Inlet's mouth.

Our light-gray swath of sand and tide flat butted up on the map against the light blue of KMm (K for the Cretaceous age, M for the Mississipian, and m for metamorphic rocks), before jumping the fjord to a lavender headland of KTrmc, where the metamorphosed sandstones were replaced by metamorphosed basalt. Tucked into a pocket, beside the topographic map that guided us, I carried a map drawn in jagged blobs and wavy slices, colored in muted blues and shades of beige, set apart by the black dashed lines of faults, the pink folds that trap oil, and the printed arrows that sought to tell me how this solid earth was moving. It was a color-by-number with brief and unpronounceable codes; decipherable only by a thick, stapled printout I kept in a drybag—the secret key of geology.

Aside from a brief fling with a seaweed guide and a colorful handbook to intertidal life, this map and its geologists' dry descriptions would be my only reading material beyond the back of a potato chip bag for the next three months. You don't start out reading potato chip bags, of course. That usually takes a few weeks. After that, it seems perfectly normal to peer at the fonts and logos, diving into animated discussions of the nutritional characteristics and marketing strategies of Kettle Chips versus Nature Valley Granola Bars. This is what you do as an explorer, when the maps have already been made.

Captain Cook had to wonder about the shape of the world. I didn't even have to wonder what was inside it. My secret key turned terse acronyms into pictures of ancient volcanoes, layered sea beds, and buckled mountains. It told a story of a land that was crumpled, folded, stretched, and towed. The geologists call it an accretionary wedge—the piece of earth that gets scraped off the ocean floor as an oceanic plate dives beneath a continental plate. Pieces of rock were dragged along the Pacific Coast from California, then discarded here, scraped and piled together at the edge of the continent. They'd moved to Alaska like I had myself—so slowly and inexorably that they'd forgotten they ever used to belong anywhere else.

Most of this region was as old as the dinosaurs. We'd scrambled on Jurassic eruptions crystallized into cliffs, worn down by millions of years of ice and waves. Katmai saw fossils of Stegosaurs and Tyrannosaurs in every boulder. Hig and I found hard white scribbles in the shale—the curls of ancient snails and the almond-shaped cross sections of clams. In the best spots, it was almost a new exercise regimen. Squats, in which you balance thirty pounds of two-year-old on your shoulders while squatting every few seconds to inspect a new cobble, increasing the workout difficulty by filling your pockets and pouches with as many rocks as can fit between the water bottles and snacks. Then you build cairns and walk away, waves lapping at those monuments to "I have too much to carry already."

The tide began to flow in. The waves lay down. Our destination—that cardboard box of food and the people holding it for us—was only across China Poot Bay. So we tied our packrafts up to the wreck we were huddled behind, unrolled them and blew them up with a nylon sack. In this crumpled, brushy country, boats have always been the way to arrive.

Walking into Kachemak Bay Wilderness Lodge, we exploded: four pairs of boots filled with sand and the two sleeping pads on top of the two coats, and the two coats for each of the kids as well, and warm puffy pants and rainpants and eight mittens, and hats and balaclavas. Soon we'd shed a pile that outmatched our paltry bodies, laying damp and colorful nylon next to boxes of broccoli and cabbage in the mud room. How nice it was to be inside where it was warm!

This lodge was built big enough and beautiful enough for tourists, in shining local wood. But right now it held only seven, my family of four, the couple who were winter caretakers, Deb and George, and their one-year-old son. Even so empty, the lodge seemed small, set against the snowy peaks and ice-crusted grass. Like us, Deb and George were here to see this place when most people don't—when it's still remote—carefully readying the lodge until it was time to swing open the doors for herds of tide-pooling school kids. In April now, those groups were still a few weeks away.

We sat on round kitchen stools, sipping cups of tea, swapping the same sorts of stories that visitors always have. We talked, full of pride and attachment, about our homes. Deb and George told us about red currants spilling over the ocean cliffs, scuttling tide pool creatures, and a rare patch of hemlock forest across the water. We told them about gathering firewood and blueberries, trips to snag salmon at the edge of the hatchery, and the tiny red octopuses that hide under rocks on the beach where Hig grew up. Although the tea was made of local nettles and the dinner was made of salmon, we didn't depend on any of it. Not really. Unlike the more ancient residents of Kachemak Bay, we had a brand-new box full of baggies of M&Ms and crackers and rice and oil. I popped a bite or two of each snack as I rearranged the packaging and tallied it all in a page at the back of my journal. It was hard to expect we'd ever feel wanting.

Lituya had seen the resupply box too. It was bedtime, and our gear and food was lumped in piles that reflected in the huge glass walls, ready to pack and leave again tomorrow. It would be a hiking day, so sleep was imperative. The kids were tucked into their sleeping bags. Lituya was actually tied into hers, hopping around the carpeted room like an angry black tube worm with a tuft of red hair, screaming "I really want chocolate!" with fierce and violent optimism. Hig pulled his sleeping bag over his ears. Katmai whined that Lituya was too loud, and that he also wanted chocolate.

I hunched over my journal. "Tomorrow. You can have more chocolate when we're hiking again."

The self-proclaimed Crazy Cephalosaurus of the Late Cretaceous banged his domed head on snow-covered deadfall, dusting his eyebrows white. From my back, excited by every lump of brown mud along the trail, Lituya watched for coyote poop. I passed out the day's ration of chocolate, then a constant stream of pretzels from a bag so new that we found some whole ones. So new the bag was free of holes. Lituya thumped her hand on my shoulder, screeching as soon as each pretzel was gone. Her plump little fingers had turned pink with the cold. I paused to hand Hig Lituya's mittens. I estimated that we spent about 20 percent of our time applying and reapplying mittens, and another 20 percent applying and reapplying snacks (which don't mix well with mittens). I considered duct tape, briefly, or Hig's more complicated system of attaching every loose end with dental floss and Aquaseal glue. A sticky Velcro mitten with different snacks adhered to each finger?

Lituya wiggled, and I released her into the path of ankle-deep snow. Katmai-the-dinosaur raced ahead, snow-skating a double line of shuffling prints, then breaking into a run before plopping down to wait for us ahead.

"Can I zoom now?" Lituya's words were muffled, as she lay face first in the snow, seemingly untroubled by the consequences of trying to keep up with her older brother. I reached down to lift her back onto her feet. She struggled to wipe her snowy mittens together, licking the dirty snowball clumps hanging off the loose threads, then continued in an awkward plunging run. The kids left their wavering lines of footsteps, grayish holes punched by dirty mittens, and bottom-scooching imprints along the snowy logs that bridged the trail—dead for decades now, from a spruce-bark beetle outbreak that had devastated much of the Kenai Peninsula. "Is this hole moose poop? Where is the moose poop? Can I step around it?"

Later, Katmai-the-dinosaur became a *Homo erectus*, making a stone hand ax to cut firewood as we sheltered in a coastal cave. His rock smashed against the firewood pile, rubbing bark off the smaller twigs. Both kids threw sticks on the fire. I plucked icicles from the cave's roof, added them to the water bottles, and rattled them impatiently, waiting for them to melt. I wanted a sip, but the few drops of liquid would help melt the rest of the ice. Water was an issue. The streams were dry or frozen. On the beach, plumes of powdery snow whirled up from the ground in wild gusts, above the tide's melt line. Smoke curled up the cave walls, billowing out above our heads, then shredding in the wind. Crouching around the blaze, with the cave's rough walls reflecting the flickering heat at my face, it was easy to pretend we were cave men—that there was nothing more in this wild world than scattered little families like ours, sheltered against the winter's cold breath.

But I'd keep the lighter and the tent all the same. I broke a few icicles into a pot. The Dena'ina—the Native group that calls Cook Inlet home—once made their fires with a strap-drill and cooked their food by dropping hot rocks in water-proof spruce-root baskets. They didn't have metal, but they had better shelter than we did, most of the time. I imagined that some traveling hunters once used this exact same spot, ducking into this cave, escaping the wind and snow. I turned to Hig, as he returned to our cave with another armful of wood. "Every day of this trip, sometimes every hour, I think—thank God I have XtraTufs," I said. "My feet are actually dry. And at this season, with the kids—how could we do this without fire?" Rubber boots and flaming wood—the things I was most grateful for in the world.

We followed the prints of snowshoe hares and lynx along an empty summer hiking trail, drifted in with snow. I chipped through the ice of the next creek to fill the water bottles. Each night I tucked them beside the sleeping bag Hig and I shared, beside the tiny wood stove that would go out as soon as Hig stopped sawing spruce limbs with the bow saw he'd made from a bent branch and a saw blade. We all fell asleep, breathing hours of frost onto our walls.

Despite the supposed progress of spring, it seemed that the land was sinking into a deeper and deeper cold. In our bedtime stories, Ziggy the Raven found fire. On the third morning beyond the lodge, a swirl of wind turned all the turquoise and black and gray into dull and roiling white. "My longest finger is cold!" Katmai complained. "The fingers on the other hand are cold too! I can't walk fast on the grass!" The knobs of brown rye grass were slicked down with a lumpy coat of salt ice. Katmai slipped down from the top of one, on his knees in the slush, face screwed up to yell again. "I can't!"

"Here." I grabbed his mitten, pulled him up to his feet, then up into my arms, hugging him awkwardly against my chest as Lituya rode on my back. It was a hunched-over stumbling sort of hurry, feeling out the slippery grass with my boots, seeking the relatively straightforward footing of the gravel shore. Slush piled up at the water's edge in soft gray ridges, slowly biting into the clean snow above. The white blanket was broken only by thin black crescent moons—unburied edges of the largest rocks. Gusts blew clouds of snow along the ground, sweeping them into funnels that raced through the trunks of the ghost forest that lined the shore.

Hig and I raced the tide around the edges of the cliffs, tugging on Katmai's mitten to hurry him, wading ankle deep around the points—Katmai lifted overhead—as the water moved in. Beyond the shelter of the last windward cliff, the air pierced my eyes, whistled ice into my nostrils, stung so fiercely I could barely even look into the storm. I could barely look at anything at all. Katmai walked backward, sideways, hollering a refusal to go any direction but straight downwind. The shrieking was in stereo—one strain from over my shoulder, the other from the end of my arm.

"It's too windy!" Lituya yelled. "Aaah! Never never! It's too windy! Aaah! Go in the trees!"

"We *are* heading for the trees! See, they're right over there! We're almost there!" The wind snatched the yells from my throat, until I wasn't sure if anyone farther away than Lituya—farther than my shoulder—could hear me at all. The world was black and white and deafeningly loud. The seagulls weren't playing in the wind anymore. Our nylon jackets and mittens were the only specks of color. We were the only animals moving.

It was terrible! Or maybe not. My brain reached out to give me a firm shove down from the intrepid horror of momentary experience—back into the realm of mundane discomfort. *No one is in any immediate danger of frostbite or hypothermia. The wind will be less intense once we get around this point. We'll have a warm fire in the stove tonight. The storm will end eventually. This is all too normal to get worked up about. As soon as the kids stop whining, I can think again.*

The rattling storm of tears and impatience rose up and broke over all of us. I braced myself against the force of those shrill whines. Even after four years of parenthood, I was more used to the wind. That's what comes of having too much experience. It takes away some drama from being caught out in a blizzard on the wrong side of a miles-wide ocean bay with almost no food. We rounded the point and entered the trees. The alders and spruce muffled the roar and the snowflakes swirled a little more gently to the ground, forming soft piles on the branches and logs we wriggled over. Lituya licked the snow from her mitten.

"It's the coldest ice age of the Pleistocene, and I'm a woolly mammoth!" Katmai declared, stomping as heavily as his small soft-soled boots would allow, raking the snow with outstretched arms. "I'm digging in the snow with my tusks to find food!"

I expected a blizzard in April. Or at least I didn't *not* expect it. Katmai, however, expected saber-toothed cats, a woolly rhinoceros, and a pack of prehistoric hunters. Why downplay your situation with boring reality? *It's not just a blizzard, it's an ice age! I'm a mammoth that never gets cold!* And he didn't. The mammoth traveled uncomplainingly, his tusks churning up spruce twigs and crunchy brown grass. What would real mammoths have eaten? Or real people, for that matter?

My stomach twinged as I unwrapped a pair of granola bars, one for each child, from the small box we'd picked up in the lodge. The blizzard delayed us. We were on the south side of Kachemak Bay, a few crinkles east of China Poot, and the next spot on the map was on the northern shore. Hig and I were hungry. Not dieting hungry or fasting hungry or I-forgot-to-pack-a-lunch hungry. The kind of hungry that most of humanity has always known, save for a few privileged modern folks, like we were most of the time. This kind of hungry was feed-your-kids-first-because-who-knows-when-we-get-food-again hungry.

April must have always been a hungry month—so close to spring but nothing yet growing. The Dena'ina called it *Nut'aq'i N'u*, or Geese Month. No geese yet in the blizzards, they would have been hunting belugas or seals, or beaver, or trout. Or waiting for the blizzard to break. A few hundred years ago, where would my family be? Hunting seals, or waiting for the men to return with fresh meat? Down at low tide, seeking chitons and clams? Cocooned in a village, feeding the fire, while eating our dwindling stores?

Archaeology leaves us such small scraps to build that story. Eight thousand years ago, people lived right here in Aurora Lagoon, in the oldest carbon-dated site in Cook Inlet. In Kachemak Bay in 5000 BC, the Kachemak Tradition people left behind petroglyphs and carved stone lamps. In 1200 AD, in Halibut Cove, the Dena'ina left the sunken pits of their houses. Seal bones and sea urchin spines crumble out of a midden on a Seldovia beach, remnants of the late 1400s. Even the more recent history is mysteriously vague. From Baranov to Portlock, the Cook Inlet of the late 1700s and early 1800s was a busy place. Explorers from several nations sailed past, mapping, trading, claiming, taking, and filling out logs with detailed notes. The Russians were encamped as close as Nanwalek. But on most of these explorers' charts, Kachemak Bay was merely a shallow dent, often cut off by the edge of the paper. When it was mentioned, the bay was only as a spot inconveniently deep for an anchor.

The north side was drawn smooth, lacking the long finger of the Homer Spit. The south side was a simple curve, missing the crinkled fjords we'd been paddling. Shelter for paddlers but without charts, they were far too dangerous for a sailing ship. And perhaps far too shallow. The glaciers pushed farther into the bay then. China Poot—the fjord we'd just crossed—was as recently as 1900 nothing but a glacier-vomited wash of stones.

Even when they skip past villages and bays, all expedition journals complain about the weather. In the summer of 1786, William Beresford—sailing from England on Captain George Dixon's ship in the hopes of developing the fur trade—noted "though this is the latter end of July, the weather is in general cool, damp, and disagreeable, with frequent showers of snow or sleet, and the surrounding prospect barren, dreary, and uncomfortable." Alaska had been gripped by the cold of the little ice age for hundreds of years by then and was only just starting to warm back up.

Certainly, I've never heard of snow here in July. As the frost crinkled in my nostrils and the snow swirled around our alderthicket camp, the one thing I knew was that the people here a few hundred years ago surely had it much worse than we did. If they could have paddled across the bay to a road system and grocery store, they might have done it. Or maybe they too would have waited out the weather.

I used the blade of a paddle to sweep as much snow as I could from the frozen dirt, then took off my mitten to tie a tent string to a convenient trunk of alder. Frozen alder leaves peeled and fractured underfoot. A few thawed, mushily, on our floor, next to the burning stove I wished I was cooking on. The kids played games with ice chipped from the water bottles I'd just filled— already mostly frozen. They ate Grape-Nuts and slushy milk for dinner, while I watched, even jumpier than usual to ensure they spilled nothing, wasted nothing. It was such a short hop from the lodge at China Poot to the next village on the northeastern shore of Kachemak Bay. It had seemed so pleasingly light to travel with only three days of food. As light as you can get. All the winter clothes on our bodies, and not a lot of extra diapers either, and even though nearly everything we owned had to fit in Hig's one huge pack, it fit just fine.

I took another bite of my own dinner—a watery broth made entirely from melted ice, a few spoonfuls of nutritional yeast, and some dried jalapenos—and wondered when the frothing surface of Kachemak Bay would settle. When we might reach civilization on the other side. The four of us cuddled into a comfortable squash of sleeping bags as the fire began to dwindle. No longer a woolly mammoth, Katmai pointed out that our family was now an Apatosaurus herd that had eaten all the trees and needed to migrate to find more food. I thought that was just about right.

Grit is caked into the tread of my Xtratuf boots, the classic Alaskan footwear.

THE APOCALYPSE PARTY

APRIL 11–16: AURORA LAGOON TO HOMER

Scattered chunks of sea ice turned into slushy mats, licking the muddy north shore of Kachemak Bay. It must have been as cold as we'd felt it was. Cold enough that the ice could float a crowd of harbor seals, fat commas with upturned tails, slinking into the water as soon as we could make out their shapes. The undersides of my legs were freezing. The top sides were warmed by the sleeping weight of Lituya. The sun bounced off the water in a dazzling blast, and I tugged her hood a little bit, trying to shield that freckled nose.

The storm had passed. As soon as the waves flattened, we pulled up the stakes from the frozen alders and launched the rafts into Aurora Lagoon. Kachemak Bay was about four miles across, and we paddled it quickly, thinking of civilization, and food, and the chances another storm might hit us on the way.

We landed as the tide rose over the last of the red and black gravel beach, and stomped our footprints into the narrow band of salty slush that remained between the ocean and the bluffs. I parceled out the last of our granola bars. It was only a mile or two to the first village—and our next supply box. The Russians were expecting us.

These aren't the same Russians who swept through this coast in the eighteenth and nineteenth centuries. The three Russian villages at the head of Kachemak Bay—Kachemak Selo, Vosnesenska, and Razdolna—burst from the sand and alders in the late 1960s. The map we carried was older than they were. These villages weren't even a dot on the map. We walked through K Selo on a dusty dirt road, past wooden houses, brown grass yards, and chickens. There were barbed-wire fences and bar grates at every driveway, like the town was built for invisible cows. It looked ancient and pastoral, with slips of Russian conversation flowing from women in long dresses and white sneakers. I stuck out like a grubby, smelly, ill-dressed adventurer, which was normal for me. But here I also stuck out like a tourist. Like a foreigner.

I'd never visited the Russian villages. I had even taken pains to avoid them. Twice before on our way to Homer from some wilderness jaunt, Hig and I had paddled past that cluster of lights that wasn't a dot on the map, making sure to be well beyond them before we landed. The villages were notoriously isolationist. I didn't want to bother anybody. I still didn't, scuffing my feet nervously on the gravel while I wondered how to make good on the invitation we had to visit an elder named Sava. K Selo didn't look like I expected. It didn't look like the newest community on the bay. Maybe because the people here didn't follow the Seldovian tradition of leaving Tyvek on the outside of your house for a decade. Maybe because I was expecting cows.

An approaching group was speaking in English, which seemed promising. "Excuse me. Do you know where Sava lives?" The trio of teachers gestured us across the street and kept walking. We knocked on the door to the arctic entry, where we pulled off our rubber boots before piling into a comfortable living room—self-conscious, muddy, and ravenous. The kids dove for the bucket of Legos beside the coffee table, which was shiny clean and graced with a basket of artificial flowers. Hig and I perched on the couch.

Mostly bald on top, with a beard that hung down in two gray tufts, Sava held forth in a thick Russian accent. He sent my mind swimming with the looping routes of his people's migration: Russia, China, Hong Kong, Brazil, Oregon, and now Alaska. All of that since 1920. How much of the world these isolated people must have seen! Sava didn't even remember Russia. His story—the story of all three Russian villages in Kachemak Bay—was the story of the Old Believers, a sect that had separated from the Russian Orthodox Church in 1666. The tsar had swept through all the holy books and rituals, changing two alleluias to three, changing "the True Lord and Giver of Life" to "the Lord, the Giver of Life," clockwise to counterclockwise, and an array of other shifts in ritual so specific it seems hard to believe, from the outside, that they could drive such a wedge. But the changes were as forceful as they were arbitrary, sweeping away the comfort of centuries-old practice with all the power of government.

Old Believers could not be tolerated by the state. Some were executed. They were persecuted, driven into isolated communities all around the world, bonded by belief, culture, and a strict set of rules. The rules, written in the seventeenth century, lay out every word to be spoken at weekly church service as well as the proper ways to dress. Sharing dishes and cups with a nonbeliever (or a church member temporarily being shunned for an infraction) is absolutely forbidden. This didn't stop Sava's wife from sweeping past to hand us a plastic clamshell package of breadsticks, then sweeping away again in a brief flurry of Russian. It's the letter of the law that's important here. Sharing food, minus the dishes, is perfectly okay. I nibbled on my pair of breadsticks as slowly as I could manage, while my stomach (still mostly running on the fumes of last night's jalapeno and yeast dinner) decided to take the cue to growl loudly for more.

Many of their traditions aren't mentioned in the rules, however. It used to be the custom for them to milk their own cows—which explained the fences and bar grates all around town. But now it isn't. There are no rules about milk in cartons—no way for any such rules to have been written. There are no rules about motor boats or telephones, or internet, or cars. Religious rituals from the 1600s, set against the backdrop of modern technology.

Stan—the Old Believer who'd contacted us over email and hooked us up with Sava in the first place—explained it all in English, after picking us up at the base of the switchbacks that connected K Selo to Voznesenka. Hig and I used to never take rides on our expeditions. "No motorized transport" is such a pleasingly pure rule. It's forced us to walk through so many inconvenient places over the years, in so much inconvenient weather. Yet no explanation of those fond memories can convince a preschooler to hike five miles out of his way to visit a total stranger. So now we take rides to visit people, and then take them right back to where we started, connecting the dots in our imaginary line. Our customs, like those of the Old Believers, can evolve with the times.

The road up from K Selo was making me rethink this particular detour. The pickup was unremarkable yet somehow seemed much too wide for the road we were traveling. I clung tightly to Katmai at each precarious corner, picturing a scenario wherein the truck tumbled off the sheer precipice on this crumbling set of switchbacks. How might the truck land? If we survived the fall, how might we escape? It's an adventurer's habit to vividly imagine the worst before proceeding. It is more helpful in planning an ocean crossing than for sitting in someone else's car. Sava had told us about this road. "The troopers tried to close it off," he shrugged, describing the home-carved route up the cliffs that was K Selo's only connection to the rest of the road system. "I told them the Russian boys would just throw the barriers off the cliff." The Russian boys, in fact, had.

Stan drove the unofficial road with an easy confidence, chatting all the way until the truck ground to a stop in the ordinary driveway of an ordinary house. Stan was a middle-aged teacher, a Santa Claus look-alike who wore the Old Believers trademark long white beard. He described himself as perhaps the only convert to the Old Believer faith. He'd married into it, but that wasn't the half of it. Stan had fallen in love with the religion as much as he had with his wife. Old Believers don't take on converts lightly. "I look at those other religions [Christian sects]," he explained, "and I think, 'They're trying, but they're so far from the right path.' Not that I have any divine inspiration, but just practically. There are things that religion is supposed to supply, and they don't supply it, or they try to in the wrong ways. This [the Old Believer faith] has been around for hundreds of years, and it works."

Stan wanted nothing more from the future than a continuation of this well-engineered system. His five kids were grown, and he hoped even those who had temporarily strayed would settle down to continue the Old Believer traditions. One of Stan's sons was already a teacher in the local school, just like Stan and his wife. When Stan was done extolling the virtues of the Old Believer religion, he paused to give us a single caveat, gleaned from a pop psychology read that topped the stack of popular science books on his living room table. "There are studies that say you value more what you worked harder to get," he said. "I had to stand at the back of church services for a year before I could join."

Humans are funny that way. We cling to the hard-won. We feel great attachment to the inconvenient, to the rules we subscribe to, and to the people who suffer through them with us. What else could bring someone like me out into the blizzards, the waves, the slush-caked beach? Out on a human-powered journey again? My family bonded in the pursuit of the inconvenient.

The crumbling curves of the K Selo switchbacks were a mark of inconvenience. Isolationism. But also toughness, resilience, a stubborn drive to create their own world to live in. The history of Alaska is full of communities built from scratch—booming and busting on the backs of newcomers who leapt into gold, coal, and a whole array of industries they knew nothing about before. The Old Believers knew nothing about the ocean, but they built themselves boats and invented themselves as fishermen. They are some of the last pioneers.

"Watch out for the asteroids!" Katmai yelled, pelting the beach with rocks. "Now no plants are growing! Dust is in the air! The dinosaurs are extinct!" The dinosaurs *were* extinct, long before these rounded cliffs of sandstone formed. We were making our way west along the northern shore of Kachemak Bay, across a geologic divide from the fjords we'd been traveling. These rocks were born here. Tens of millions of years ago, rivers spilled sand across broad river deltas on the edge of Cook Inlet, capturing fallen leaves and chunks of wood into layers of coal and leaving delicate impressions of the leaves in the sand.

"Do you want a pancake?" Lituya asked. She gripped two flattish rocks in her puffy red mittens. "I'm putting maple syrup on them, and molasses on them." She carefully patted a pile of muddy slush onto the top of each rock. "And now I'm baking them in my pan!" Setting them on top of a larger boulder, she squatted down to stare at her creations.

"Sure, I'd love one!" I called back. "Bring it here!" I was standing a few dozen yards ahead of her, kicking the cobbles with the toe of my boot, absently looking for fossils. I spent quite a lot of time standing a few dozen yards ahead of one or the other of my children. I considered it a prime "coaxing distance"—close enough to converse in a loud voice but far enough that the child in question would be tempted to narrow the gap.

This was step six in our usual fourteen-step cycle: Lituya would wiggle her legs against my torso, proclaiming, "I want to walk!" (1), run along the beach for a short distance until a patch of mud flattened her across it (2), grudgingly accept a shoulder ride over a rough area while smearing her muddy mittens across my face (3), run again (4), walk along chattering and holding my hand (5), find something interesting to play with (6), find something else interesting to investigate (7), respond to my pleas for forward motion with a "But I need to [make rock pancakes, ride this airplane log, draw pictures in the sand] a little more!" (8), walk a bit (9), ask for a snack (10), walk a bit more (11), agree to be wrapped onto my back again (12), ask for another snack (13), then fall asleep (14), sometimes with a potato chip in her mouth. This cycle would repeat until bedtime.

Katmai was a little farther ahead with his dad, repeating a fairly similar cycle with a little bit faster forward momentum, no rides or naps, and rather longer periods of unrelenting dissertations on the latest product of his imagination. Do you know all about Pasture Mice and Glacier Mice and their fantastic machines with rockets and wheels and candy-makers? I certainly do.

Lituya on my back again, I caught up to Hig and Katmai, picking their way through the tide-packed slush at the top of the beach. "I'm really looking forward to having an easy walking day," Hig commented, pulling his boot out of a knee-deep hole, then reaching back to lift Katmai out of the hole, "to see how that will go. I have every reason to believe it will happen in the future, but—"

"We've had a couple of easy *paddling* days," I pointed out.

"And some not."

I agreed, pulling my own boot out of a different knee-deep hole. We were only about two weeks into the journey, after all. Hardly even time to get into the swing of things. Far above us, the road system sprawled out above the bluff, connecting Homer to its suburban homesteads and to the Russian villages we'd just left behind. We could see none of it. The sandstone bluffs that walled us off from the road were gold and gray in the sun, streaked with layers of glistening black coal. The beaches themselves were black with wave-crumbled coal, speckled with the gleaming shells of moon snails, tiny pink clams, cockles, and whelks. Glacier-dropped boulders stood like monuments on the tide flats, reflected in the pools of mud. On the south side of Kachemak Bay, the one we'd just come from, everything shone snow white from the blizzard. It sure was pretty in the light.

I couldn't really remember what it had looked like the last two times I'd followed this beach into Homer. Both times were near midnight, at the end of a day of more than twenty miles of walking, in some crazy last-day push to just get the whole trip over with. We hadn't stopped in the Russian villages. On one of those occasions, I remembered, Hig actually fell asleep on his feet. I poked him, over and over again with my walking stick, so he wouldn't trip over the boulders. On another trip here (or was it the same one?), I remember nothing much beyond a burning craving for Chinese food.

Mini dust storms swirled in every crumbling gully, spitting piles of small rocks onto the beach. I picked up a chunk of clay fired orange from an ancient underground coal fire and scrawled a smiling cartoon face on a boulder. "See, like chalk," I showed the kids. Hig looked for geologic faults. The tide had dropped to leave us a path between the ocean and the cliffs, swept clean of snow. Despite the kids' slow pace—or because of it—this *was* easy.

The ambition of an adventurer can quickly become a trap. Once you start moving past bumbling idiocy (maybe those first few months huddling under a silver-sided tarp in a homemade fleece sleeping bag on cold dirt), there's an irresistible force that begins to pull you outward. Bigger! Faster! Longer! Wilder! Eventually, something has to give. Do you push for ever faster records or ever riskier challenges? Hang up your laurels and forever be known as the people who did that thing, back in the day? Or do you just keep going? Every great journey is an experience-of-a-lifetime. Hig and I must be greedy to collect so many of them.

Homer greeted us with almonds and fruit (brought down to the beach by new friends of friends) and the pervasive scent of dog crap (piled up through all the layers of winter snow, now thawing in a great brown rush as the sun angled in from the south). I bit down on a California strawberry and followed a six-year-old up the scrambling trail to his house. This was only the first of three houses we planned to stay in during our few days in Homer—each one conveniently placed a kids' day walk beyond the next. It was the seventh house we'd slept in on the trip so far. They were friends of friends, just like everyone else in Alaska.

The entire state functions rather like a geographically enormous small town. Sit down and spend a few minutes with a new acquaintance, and you'll soon discover that someone you visited on the Arctic Ocean once fished with them in Bristol Bay. Or their college friend waited tables with your sister-in-law. One degree of separation. In Homer it was even more extreme. Homer's the place Seldovians go when they need a bit more civilization. Seldovia's the place Homerites go when they need a little less. We were pretty much neighbors already.

Homer was named after a con man, after a cluster of disused buildings where a man called Homer Pennock left his name and his investment partners' cash. He landed in 1896 with fifty miners, and within a year he was gone to the Klondike. Other miners worked the coal that lines the Homer bluffs, and they even built a railroad between those shores and the end of Homer's long sand spit. The money never panned out. The new town didn't even last ten years. By 1905 only a lonely caretaker stood guard over the crumbling buildings at the end of the spit.

Eventually, homesteaders came in. They picked up some of the coal on the beach, and threw it in their stoves, but mostly they grew vegetables. Agriculture wasn't a money maker either, but it didn't matter, because those swamps and spruce forests and mountain sunrises had gotten into their blood. Some of the homesteaders stayed, fishing and building, and figuring things out, until the arrival of the highway in 1950 firmly cemented Homer's place as the center of local civilization. Today, rednecks and hippies gather together in Homer at the end of the road, in a town known for its artists and sports fishing, where a few rainbow-painted school busses park between the trucks and RVs. It was a perfect place for an apocalypse party.

I followed the driveway past a pair of giant high-tunnel greenhouses, draped in white. His and hers greenhouses, then a sweep of gardens, their dark soil frozen in waiting for massive Brussels sprouts. For kale and turnips and cabbage and beets and all the cold-weather beauties. I ascended a set of wooden steps right into Kyra and Neil's living room. Neil is an encyclopedia of agricultural knowledge and tinkering skills, and after a few minutes of conversation, I felt like he was going so fast, I ought to be taking notes. I want to jot down Kyra's words as well. She holds forth in a loud, animated voice and can talk about anything. She seems to know everyone—at least one expert in every conceivable field.

A childless couple with a house they say is too big for them, Neil and Kyra are longtime sustainability and local-food advocates. Their garden is considerably larger than the house (it's hard to escape a visit without a bag of vegetables). A trapdoor in the living room opened to welcome visitors to the upstairs guest rooms. Guests trickled into their living room. Writers and fishermen, organizational leaders and educators, friends, acquaintances, and strangers. Kyra had invited people who were willing to speculate about the future. We poured ourselves drinks, answered the usual questions about blizzards, children, rafts, and adventure, and then Kyra called the room to order.

The chatter dropped as we asked our question: "What is the future of this place—in fifty or a hundred years?" The answers flowed quickly. These folks were prepared.

"A crash is inevitable."

"We are adaptable but not exempt from suffering and extinction. Not all our needs will be met."

"Without cheap energy, people will be fighting for food."

"Science has been depressing me frequently lately."

Their gestures were animated. Heartfelt opinions supported with a dramatic wave of a pizza slice. Glasses rattled against tables and counters, and ideas rattled against the windows. Doomsday filled the air. How many people believe we're headed for collapse? Hig carefully clarified the terms: a substantial world population decline in the next fifty to one hundred years. Nearly 40 percent of the guests raised their hands.

Another pizza appeared. A crash of home-grown vegetables on a sizzling crust. This portable pizza oven was Neil's latest project, and he'd never used it before. We were the guinea pigs for the hungry guests at next summer's farmers market. The pizzas tasted fresh and cheery, each one different from the last. Each pizza was a flat earth of limitless possibilities.

Facts peppered the conversation. Carbon dioxide concentrations in the atmosphere. Salmon swimming through streams that already waver into dangerous heat. And so many people. "We talked more about the population problems in the 1970s than we do now," one man lamented. "Population *times* consumption," someone else pointed out. People spoke loudly, with the intensity of someone rubbernecking at a car crash, their voices sparkling with the secret thrill of disaster. The bigger the better, in some ways. Pompeii and the fiery crash that killed the dinosaurs. The floods and storms that spawned our greatest myths. The zombie flicks and the thousand different imaginings of a postapocalyptic world—infected, flooded, mutated, scorched. Disaster is easiest to imagine when it's sudden and total—canned foods and machine guns in the basement style—so big you can't possibly think of anything else. Until then, we eat pizza.

"When I was young," one woman said, "I thought that by the time I was forty, there would be no universe. We would have blown each other up by now. But I turned forty and there was the universe, dealing with many of the same problems it was when I was young." Another said: "There have been generations that knew nothing but war. In the future, there may be times that are uncomfortable—awful even—for generations. But things will eventually settle out and work out." And this final comment, which seemed beautiful and awful in equal measure: "Our job is to share joy and hope as we degrade."

Environmental disasters feeding back into economic collapse. Climate change and pollution and resource depletion. That's what most people at the party were worried about, and that kind of disaster isn't like a nuclear holocaust or a global pandemic. Nothing so flashy. Maybe just generation upon generation of hard times. People have short memories. We're ungrateful little bastards and we always want more because we've forgotten what life was like a few years ago before we acquired our latest convenience.

It was just a few years ago that we got running water at our Seldovia home. I remember chipping a hole in the ice, balancing on a pair of logs in boots and ice cleats as I dangled a jar on a string over our shallow well. I remember the *slop-slop-slop* of staggering down the driveway with a pair of buckets, trip after trip just for one day of watering the garden. It was just a few years ago but already retreating into the haze of a past I didn't want to return to. Short memories work the other way too. Someone in Neil and Kyra's living room launched into a description of a study that had been done on a particular sport fishery—year after year of triumphant pictures, and year after year those fish got smaller, until forty years later the trophy fish were half the size. But the fishermen's smiles were just as big.

Scientists call this a "shifting baseline." It means that people aren't really listening to Grandpa's fishing stories. Instead, we measure against our own experience. Scientists measure against the first year they have quantitative data for. And over the gap of generations, we forget how it used to be. We don't know what we're missing. But we know what we have. "Alaska has a lot of resilience," one guest said. "It's not that long ago that we grew our own gardens and traded with neighbors." Another offered: "I don't think salmon are forever. But if I can grow my own food and seeds . . ." A final hopeful thought: "Survival instincts will kick in at some point."

I put down my pencil for a moment, ran my finger over the cornmeal crumbs that had fallen from the pizza crust and licked them from my fingers. Expedition eating habits die hard, even here. The kids clung to my legs, exhaustion beginning to slip into whining. People spoke of adaptability, of resilience, of hope. Alaska thinks it's special, and maybe we have to. It's fun to scoff at Alaskan provincialism. At the puffed-up pride new Alaskans lord over the newest Alaskans. "You've been here one winter? I've been here *two*!" But I love Alaska as fiercely as any other newcomer. It's the best place in the world, and maybe we're special enough to keep it that way. Maybe hope requires a little bit of magical thinking. Just not quite so much that we sit back and have another beer and wait for the techno-wizards to blast us all to a brand-new planet.

Hig wished them all goodnight. Raised his glass. "Onward, to a bright apocalypse."

The next morning I ducked into of one of those vaulting greenhouses and stuck my hands wrist-deep into the warm dirt. Under the white roof I could take my coat off and pretend it was spring. A couple I'd never met before knelt beside the raised beds, planting. "Our son moved up here," said the woman, Lori, explaining their recent move from Georgia as she handed me a six-pack of seedlings. "Climate change changed the summers," her husband added, "and we were tired of intolerant people." She nodded. "We wanted community."

It seemed a good place for that. Kyra and Neil were as generous with their greenhouses as they were with everything else, loaning planting space to people who had none of their own. Katmai balanced on the wooden edges of the empty raised beds, leaping edge to edge across the greenhouse. Lituya stuck her fist in the dirt, wiped the smear of mud across her cheeks. I cradled the baby Swiss chard, those thin red stems more colorful than anything I could imagine in the half-thawed breath of April.

"Hey kids, you want to try?" I offered up a pair of seedlings, holes I'd already scooped. Most work, even dirt work, was easier to do without kids, but they should learn. The day before, a Homer mom had shown me her own pots of seedlings in the window, each a scraggle of stem with a single pair of hopeful leaves. Our kids had run and played with her slightly older ones. The mom had waved her hands across the clatter of kids and toys. "We'll be leaving them a messed-up world. They'll need skills like gardening, fishing, sustaining themselves. They'll need that connection to the land, and they'll also need to be technologically savvy. They'll need to be really smart. They'll need to walk in both worlds."

"Not *yet!*" Katmai whined when I tried to coax him out of the greenhouse. "One more jump!"

I stood by the door, wrap dangled over my shoulder ready to catch up Lituya, fanny pack buckled for a walk to the grocery store, to a friend's house, to the beach, and then away from Homer, to the next river, the next tide, the next town, the next story. Neil and Kyra's greenhouse mud left brown circles on the knees of my rainpants that froze and peeled off as we walked back into the winter air. We walked to the end of Homer's pavement and back onto the beaches, until the next town at Anchor Point, where we'd repeat the cycle, seesawing between empty and inhabited lands. We walked in as many worlds as possible.

As we depart Homer, Hig and I leave tracks across the quivering silt of the tide flats.

THE ROCKS COME TUMBLING DOWN

APRIL 17–23: HOMER TO NINILCHIK

The snails painted muddy curlicues on the rocks. I stepped heavily on their tracks, smearing the sole of my boot across their cursive trails. I reached down to give my waist belt another cinching tug. The giant brick of food and water squished a little closer to my hips. So much of life is devoted to food. Shopping! Gardening! Prepping! Cooking! Dishes! Although we had neatly sliced out several of these chores by taking off on an expedition (and committing to cook the morning coffee in the vaguely rinsed-out remains of the previous night's dinner), we'd added the even more ridiculous chore of calculating and physically carrying every bit of every meal along with us. Images of everything I might consume for the next few months seared my eyeballs. I was still woozy from late-night prep, tearing open packages of rice and crackers and nuts, pouring them into plastic bags, balancing each in my palm to estimate its weight.

I have an unusual skill with these estimations. Give me a mountain of ragged Ziplocs with crumbs and powders and half-eaten bars, and I'll add them up for you. By quarter pounds and half pounds, piling them up into an estimate of how many days it might take to devour these scraps. I'll do it when we're ten days into a fourteen-day walk, wondering how much dinner we can afford to eat. I'll do it when everything's shiny new, piling those bags into cardboard boxes, each one tallied and checked off, knowing that sleepy mistakes might leave us with far too much to carry or far too little to eat. Or perhaps a sickening glut of granola bars, almost nothing to flavor our dinners, or worse yet—not enough coffee.

I had slathered each box in duct tape, labeling each with the name of a remote spot in giant black letters. This one for a pilot, that one for a barge operator, another for the manager of a high-end lodge. We wouldn't see any of it for months. None of it gleamed as bright as the two stiff fillets of frozen salmon—a gift from a friend—tucked into the outside of Hig's pack and thawing in the morning sun, a pair of jewels in vacuum-sealed plastic.

Town—Homer—receded behind us. The morning sun slanted in from the south, touching the bluffs to create a glittering sparkle of frozen mud. Brown waterfalls gushed over the edges, fanning out into soupy filigrees—viscous fingers creeping slowly down toward an ocean they couldn't quite reach. Katmai waded experimentally into one of the deltas, pulling each foot out with a long *schluuuuk!* sound. He stared at the mud-coated boot, admiring its new decoration, then turned around to walk right through again. "It's a Cold Lava Eruption!"

I left slow, duck-footed steps in the tracks of four-wheelers and fat-tired bikes and pickup trucks making forays for the coal that tumbles down from the bluffs. We walked past their curving U-turns, each set peeling off to return to the road access, miles behind us. The last tracks turned, and we were alone again.

Dipping greasy fingers into a plastic snap-together bowl, eating fire-seared salmon that was barely cooked in the center. The cliffs dropped icy shadows on our camp.

"I'm Lead-the-way-a-saurus!" Katmai cried the next morning. "Follow me!" He leaped from one boulder to the next. He slipped, plunging butt-first into a tide pool with a loud splash and a fit of giggles. Beyond our reef, seals slept balanced on the tips of half-submerged rocks. Others were punctuated splashes, diving for fish. Young brown-headed eagles tore at carrion in the tide line, while others perched on leafless cottonwoods, turning their heads as we walked past.

"This is my horsie!" Lituya yelled. Feet on one sideways alder branch, arms stretched out above to another branch barely in reach, she jumped and jumped until the whole tree shuddered with the rhythm of thirty bouncy pounds.

"This is my airplane," Katmai contributed from a nearby toppled tree. "Where do you want to go in it?" Whatever answer I was about to invent was interrupted by a great rumbling crash. A burst of ravens squawked in the echoes—their black shapes peeling up and swirling against the golden sandstone. A smaller, more distant rumble echoed against the cliffs. Somewhere, rocks were sliding.

The bluffs were shrugging off the icy glue of winter, shivering like a person who's been cold for so long that he only notices when he finally starts to warm up. Pebbles clattered down through dripping mud. Boulders shook loose from the cliffs and rolled across the sand below. I squatted down beside one bucket-sized rock. Dark plates of Pleistocene wood peeled away in my hand, black as the coal seams but softer, like a rotten stick. A piece of the ice age, spit out by spring. We retreated back to the water's edge. It seemed safer there.

The tide claims most of this beach. Spring tides can swallow it whole, licking the base of the cliffs with an erosive salty tongue. The rock is soft here. Young and uncertain, this rock has never traveled, never endured the depths of the earth. It is mud squeezed and shaped like a potter's unbaked bowl. A few gullies carve notches into the layered stripes—woven through cotton-wood trunks and the leafless twist of alders. This early in spring, the streams that ran in those gullies were as thick and brown as chocolate milkshakes—a slurry of silt and mud. I stalked the upper beach with a cup, carefully scooping the whitest snow I could find. We had to drink something. Melt enough cheese on dinner, and you'll never notice the gray.

Yet gullies were important. As arresting as the geology might be, I had no desire to get clonked in the head by any of it. We'd just passed a fridge-sized boulder that had clearly rolled across the beach more recently than the car tracks it obliterated. Hig had been examining the remains of a massive landslide (a couple of years old) when that first crash had sent the ravens flying. So gullies—the only spots where no cliffs loomed over us— were important. Gullies were our lunch breaks. Our campsites. Havens where we could zip ourselves in and be sure nothing would tumble down upon us in the night.

Some of the men who had come on Homer Pennock's ship ended up on these beaches. There was gold on these shores. Tiny dusty motes in the dusty gritty beach, the same sort of gold that had sent men into a fever of panning and sluicing on the beaches of Nome and Turnagain and a hundred other middle-of-nowhere coasts. In 1890 the census taker had found three white men here on the beach, below a small Native settle-ment, beside a two-mile ditch they'd dug to wet their sluices, sifting through the gravel thrown up by the tides. Each time the tide dropped, the miners would drag their sluices down to the beach, move the rocks that the ocean had pushed in their way, and work for a few hours. Then they had to drag the heavy con-traptions back up the bluffs on ladders or through the narrow gullies that made their way down to shore. The men stopped when winter froze their ditch, and when summer sucked it dry. You could earn seven dollars a day at this. It might have seemed good at the time, but it was so much work, and the people soon retreated—to a better gold rush, or Outside (where they came from). Or they simply stopped scrambling down those bluffs every day and found a way to stay on top.

People here lived near the ocean, but not on the shore. This was never a maritime place. The waters of Kachemak Bay are clear. Head north—around the corner of Anchor Point—and the ocean swirls as thick and gray-brown as the streams. Just barnacles and mussels in the tide pools. Captain Cook himself refused to even call it an ocean. He left the entire inlet—the gaping fifty-five-mile-wide mouth and the entire great tidal rush of it—marked as an unnamed river. Ridiculous. But if you squint, you can see it does sort of look like one—as if the gray roil of a glacial river was supersized to flood through a valley of giants.

The people here weren't maritime folk—not in the same way the Alutiiq were. For the past thousand years, Cook Inlet has been home to the Dena'ina—Athabaskans who came to the inlet along its rivers and valleys, inland people brought to the shore—with a chain of relationships that stretches all the way through interior Alaska and Canada and all the way down to the Navajo in the Lower 48. They had boats, of course, and plenty of skill on the water. They set up in the best spots at river mouths, fishing for salmon and hunting on land. They hunted belugas and fatty seals and otters (at least so long as the Russians were wanting them). Along Alaska's coast, the ocean is where the calories are, and the Dena'ina knew it. But they never abandoned their other sources of food. They hunted everything, keeping one foot firmly on the land.

Captain Cook named Anchor Point with the hubris of a traveler—as if what he did at this spot; the fact that he anchored—was the most important thing about it. Here, the Anchor River carves a path through the bluffs, and beach sand kisses the pavement of the farthest west road in North America's sprawl of road system. If I were naming things like an explorer, I'd call it Grocery Store Point.

I rolled out of bed on yet another frigid morning, heading for a rendezvous with civilization. No I didn't. You can't *roll* out of a sleeping bag. I wriggled and scooted my upper body out of that pillowy blue down, shifted the edge of my fleece hat up over my eyes, and blinked in the gray light that filtered through the tent's walls.

This was our winter tent. One layer of dark green nylon on the outside and another layer of white nylon beneath it. It was a modern teepee—floorless, large, and round, staked out into a twelve-foot circle. One of our packraft paddles reached up at a jaunty 80-degree angle to support the roof. Right beside it, a squat titanium cylinder perched on tiny titanium legs, thrusting its collapsible titanium chimney through a hole in the roof. No envelope of nylon could hold heat over a night, but once we started a fire in it, this place would be warm. I'd mailed our summer tent to Kenai—fewer than ten days away. I wasn't at all sure I was ready to give this one up. I *love* our tent.

It's easy to become emotionally entangled with your hiking gear. You don't love a tent like you love a favorite sweater or your most useful kitchen gadget. You love it like it's your most reliable childhood friend, the shoulder you cry on when everything collapses, the only scrap of salvation and comfort in a harsh cold world. Each piece of gear we carried brought forth an outburst of emotions. You can also hate hiking gear. You can hate that leaking raincoat like a roommate who never cleans the bathroom and always breaks your favorite mugs (but you can't afford the rent without him)—inescapable and necessary and utterly maddening.

I slithered carefully, trying not to disturb Katmai where he'd crawled into our double bag sometime in the middle of that frigid night. I grasped for Lituya, who was making half-awake whimpers, partly out of her own bag. I nursed her for a few minutes until she fell asleep again and carefully tucked her in beside Hig and Katmai as I pulled myself out of that communal pile of warmth, contemplating socks.

The socks I was contemplating were gray C-shaped sculptures of frozen sweat, carefully draped over the tops of my rubber boots. I was supposed to put them on. Just one of those rules, you know. Put on the wet dirty socks every morning, so you can save the clean dry ones for sleeping in. Carrying more than two pairs is impractical. I picked up one sock, poked its toe experimentally, feeling the frost crunch between my fingers. I placed it on top of the pile of firewood near the cold stove in the middle of our tent. Who cares? No rivers to cross between here and the store at Anchor Point. How much damage could a few miles do to those fluffy clean socks? I went for it.

Flakes of frost peeled off onto my hood. The tent zipper sounded way too loud. It wasn't windy yet. No crashing waves, no squealing children, and even the seagulls and eagles were holding their tongues. The morning seemed so quiet it was almost unnerving. I didn't know if the store was even open, but I hoped I could get there, get food, and get back before anyone woke up. My legs stretched out to a full adult stride, crunching on snow and gravel. I was the only living thing on this highway.

Katmai's eyes and mouth popped open as soon as I slipped back in the tent. "Today is the day with ice cream!" he screeched.

"Ice cream!" Lituya yelled, squirming across Hig's lap, toward the pile of grocery shopping I was tossing out of the pack.

Ice cream—that most coveted yet impossible-to-pack food—had become the promise of civilization. Every time we reach a town, you get ice cream! Hig and I had used the bribe quite effectively the previous day, the thought of that melting wet sweetness enough to power a few more miles. Hig fed another chunk of wood into the fire. I rustled out the spoons and forks. They were coated in cheese from last night's dinner, and I used my teeth to peel it off. Then we sat around the stove on a twenty-degree morning, passing around a pint of peach cobbler ice cream for breakfast, before beginning our day of hiking.

It had been almost warm up at the grocery store, where the highway snaked along on the top of the bluffs. Down here the wind poured out of the inlet, catching against the cliffs, funneling along that narrow strip of beach. I snugged up the cord on the back of my hood to stop it from blowing off.

"Mom, do you know about Pasture Mice? They have machines with *eighteen* wheels! And skis, and stabbers, and . . ." Skeletal remains of cod lined the beach, draped across a curving wrack line of seaweed and wood. "And there are Pasture Turtles too, and their shells are sometimes purple, but sometimes green, and . . ."

A bald eagle screeched its twittering cry from overhead. Another one—even smaller and squeakier—replied from over my shoulder. Then it followed up with a giggle. "I'm a bird riding on my mama bird!" Lituya loved to watch the birds, imitating their cries.

Water spit out from under the edge of the frozen Anchor River. Not much water. The shivering melt that sent rocks tumbling down the bluffs was still only skin-deep—the thaw hadn't penetrated the hills and mountains and valleys full of snow. We crossed on the ice. We threaded a cautious single file line that reminded me of an aerial photograph I'd seen—zoomed out above the migrating caribou until they were nothing but dotted brown lines on a blue-white world. Katmai spun twirling circles on the frozen pools along the banks. Beneath the layer of fleece pants, puff pants, and rainpants, I'm not even sure he could feel when he fell on his butt.

The caribou were moving. We were moving. I planned and I wrote, and I tried to mold pithy funny answers for the "why?" people always asked us, but maybe it was just as primal for us as the caribou. Tugged across the landscape by an invisible and inescapable force that rendered us powerless in its grip. Just keep moving. Keep traveling.

The kids climbed the roots of a tumbled-down spruce tree. Left a sandwich wedged in a crack. Nudged it with a sandy mitten. Tumbled it onto the beach. "Don't get sand in our food!" I took off my own sandy mittens to carefully peel off the edges of the sandwich and wiggled my back against the knobby weave of the root plate (the shallow lateral growth of tree roots), massaging the muscles tightened by the weight of all that kid and food. I crunched down on the remains of smooth peanut butter, rubbery store-bought bread, and the teeth-jolting bits of wave-worn sand. You could almost imagine they were nuts.

All the logs were spruce; they each looked the same. The north is a species-impoverished world. Vast tracts of wild land, but spruce is one of the few trees here. The Dena'ina didn't even classify trees by species. Spruce trees were named by the places they grew and the hardness of their wood. Practical things.

Today was plain gravel underfoot and an icy wind in the eyes. Stay away from those waves. You can't lose the mittens, and you can't afford to get them wet. Dirty snow melts to grit between your teeth. Miles behind and miles ahead look exactly the same. Even the beach trash—the orange foam that seems to go on forever.

Beaches are a kid's natural habitat, at least for my two. Run! Climb! Dig! Build! The gooey mud is perfect for smearing on every rock, the buoys are perfect as soccer balls, and how could you find a better jungle gym than a pile of wave-washed boulders? The kids ran back and forth to escape the small foamy crash of each little wave, then Lituya plopped down at the edge, giggling and laughing as her too serious older brother tried to rescue her from the tide.

Or not. We got cold rain. Blowing sleet. Miles of monotony. "What if we went through the frozen marshes instead?" Hig mused at our lunch break, throwing another stick on the fire. The flames leapt sideways, roaring in their wind tunnel, devouring the driftwood without a puff of smoke. "What if we borrowed some skis and followed the snow machine trails we saw on that map? It would be out of this wind—and maybe more variety . . ." It was the boredom that got him. Hig was too stoic to complain about the cold and the rain, but too restless and optimistic to accept any terrain that he wasn't excited about. Wondering when the sleet might stop wasn't the right kind of mystery. Coaxing the kids another mile on the sand wasn't the right kind of challenge. The grocery store at Ninilchik would have the same sorts of treats as the one at Anchor Point, and in between, the coast stretched before us, unremarkably the same.

"Every trip has a spot like this," I reminded him. "At least a couple days of regret, when you start to wonder if you ought to have planned an entirely different trip in an entirely different season, and it feels like this particular challenge will last forever. Anyway . . . just look at them." The tiny passenger lined up behind the pilot on a driftwood plane, the shrieky roars of their sound effects competing with the wind. "*They're* not bored."

We tossed the remains of the fire into the ocean. Black wood steamed, sending misty curls toward the mouth of the inlet. We'd been told—once we got here—that the north wind blows down the inlet all winter and spring. We'd been told—too late for trip planning—that when we reach the head of the inlet around May, it should switch directions, blowing from the south all summer long. We had lined ourselves up for three months of headwinds. We should have known better. A Native elder we'd met near the beginning of the journey had told us how the information age would make everything easier. We can adapt— to anything nature can throw at us or what we throw at each other—because "People don't have to just learn things by doing them anymore. They can just go to the workshop. Just read it online." If you remember to ask the right question. But who wants to know they'll have wind up their nostrils for months? Better to believe in a land of fortunes.

Alaska's attraction, for its newcomers, has always been the promise that this place can deliver what you've spent your life looking for, that it's not like anywhere else. Toss aside your concerns because everything up here is bigger and better than you can imagine, and it's there for the taking. So come and get rich. On sea otter skins, on gold and coal, on fish and oil. Come and hook the biggest fish, shoot the biggest bear. Get rich on mountain climbs or breathless paddles along fjord-crumpled coasts. Get rich on adventure, get rich for real. Get what you came for.

The 1869 *Coast Pilot* crowed that "Cook's Inlet is the great boast of the Russian navigators and authorities as the best part of Alaska, and has been favorably noticed by nearly all the old discoverers." But those old discoverers' opinions were grouchy and fickle. Captain Vancouver railed in 1794 about the excessively troublesome ice that kept them "in a continued state of impatience and solicitude." How dare a narrow escape of broken cables and grinding ice be followed by stagnant air that wouldn't fill the ship's sails? Nature, clearly, was "ungrateful to our feelings." William Beresford, on Captain George Dixon's ship, complained in 1786 about the horrid cold wet weather and summed it up this way: "So much at present for the *promised land.*"

When the sleet blew sideways and the waterfalls rushed louder and the crumpled towels of seaweed grew fat from the rain until I couldn't even tell where the tide line was, but I had to know because I was tired of tucking my dripping cold nose into my collar and wanted to find a place above the tide to camp—I understood what Beresford meant. When the weather was better, the ships' logs were as well; barrels of flashing salmon, promising turns in the coastline, cheaply bought furs of great luxury, and thick seams of coal. My journals were the same. When the mountains glitter and the eagles cry, you suddenly remember that you only had a single day of rain. Romance and adventure. Ups and downs, highs and lows. Grand fantasies, dashed hopes, crushing misery, and occasional wild success. Who could feel neutral about this place?

Seki shows Lituya the birds at her blufftop poultry farm.

SQUEEZED BY THE ROAD

APRIL 24–30: NINILCHIK TO NIKISKI

Hig bent over like some beleaguered fairy-tale character, a hunch-backed laborer staggering under his load. He ducked under the tent, upended his pack, and sent a dust cloud billowing around a rattling crash of gravel. He went for another load. I kicked the gravel into a mostly even layer, an armful of cobbles in my arms. Katmai carried the largest rocks he could, one at a time, *stomp-stomp-stomping* them into the muck. Lituya's baby-doll pretend voice was even squeakier than her ordinary one. She and the plastic baby played on a raft in the middle of the chaos.

"We don't usually need to build a cobblestone floor." I laughed self-consciously, explaining myself to our guest who had come from thousands of miles away. This guest, a journalist who wanted to understand Alaska, had brought a tent with a floor. We were the ones who were supposed to know what we were doing. Our floor would be cobblestone tonight. The highway was creeping in on us.

We'd been on this journey for about a month, and we'd only set foot on the highway a couple of times, resupplying in Anchor Point and Ninilchik. But its thrum had entered my dreams. Following us, paralleling us ever since we'd left Homer, roaring unseen from the top of the bluffs as we wound our way along the bottom. Often we could hear it, and sometimes I could even see the tops of the semitrucks—truncated rectangles sliding past in a disembodied rush.

Now those bluffs that guarded our beach had dropped until they were nothing more than steep slopes of grass, and the houses crept in on their heels. They seemed to glower down with dark glassy eyes, saying, "Here we are now. People belong behind these walls, and what are you doing out there? Out there you have nothing to sleep on." The high tide licks the bluffs, and there might be a few sticks of driftwood in someone's yard, but the only place we could find to camp was a wide switchback in an eroding dead-end road. So we squeezed the tent right across the middle of thawing muck—like a driveway abandoned under snow for the winter where everyone knows not to drive on it until it's had a few weeks to dry out.

The mud froze overnight—beneath our cobblestone floor and at the top of the beach, but it shone and jiggled at the edge of low tide, where clam diggers hunched over with five-gallon buckets and bright puffy jackets. The morning was brilliant and icy and rattled with a cold wind, and since they hadn't been camping on our road, any one of those clam diggers had a house they might have stayed inside. But they didn't. The highway brought them down to the beach. The wind flew up our nostrils and sent tatters of dried seaweed hop-tumbling across the sand, as billowing whirlwinds lashed at our ankles. Those were Hop-a-sauruses and Dust-a-sauruses, as the boulders were Slug-a-sauruses, named by our Lead-the-way-a-saurus, because even the smallest thing is grander when you call it a dinosaur.

Glittering floes of candle ice jostled their way down the Kasilof River. They washed up on the beach, shattering into glassy sticks on drifted-up whale vertebrae, on pilings, and on the tops of retaining walls meant to keep those waves at bay. The morning's tide was the lowest of the month, and the afternoon's was the highest. It pushed up the inlet, battling the wind that pushed down, tugging and shoving the water into tight brown curls topped with white. We danced in the wavering space between the waves and walls and ice, water sloshing up into our shoes when we timed it wrong.

That journalist was reporting on Alaska, not on us. He might have chosen to keep his feet dry. He might have chosen someplace other than this April-brown beach below bluffs and highway. But he didn't. Six or seven miles went by like nothing. We were patient, sure, but walking that long at four-year-old speed seemed to require far less creativity than it had only a week earlier. On our overview map—the one that showed the impossible distance of our entire route—it looked like we were actually getting somewhere.

As we walked north, the towns grew closer together, clinging to the banks of the rivers that snaked across the Kenai Peninsula flats. We'd passed Anchor Point, Clam Gulch, and Ninilchik already and were headed to pick up food in Kasilof. Kasilof is a dog-mushing town—a web of trails and roads sprawling inland through forests killed by the spruce-bark beetle a few decades ago. We hitched a ride to town, where the journalist left us, and when we made our way back down to the river mouth with all of our shopping, we found a trio of mushers in a truck, cigar smoke curling out the window. They'd been scouting the fishing. Too much ice still for herring nets.

"I like to do my adventures with dogs," the guy in back commented, as Hig's pack cratered into the sand with a thud, and I unwound the long ribbon of red fabric that attached Lituya to my back.

I smiled. Our load did make the idea of someone else pulling it seem attractive. Lituya smiled too. She knew the drill by now, instructing me from over my shoulder when new people showed up. "You go to talk. And you say: This is Lituya. And this is Katmai. And this is Erin. And this is Daddy. Now take the wrap out and show them how it works."

The guy who spoke up didn't have kids, but he was curious how we carried them. I don't have dogs, but I was curious about his mushing journeys. He'd done the math. The Iditarod race—support, checkpoints, dog food moved for you for a reasonable entry fee—was the best deal you could get for a mushing vacation. Who needs to win, when you can have an adventure? I don't smoke and I barely fish, and I think dogs are okay, but I'd rather not take care of them myself. I'd barely met these people, but it was easy enough to connect to the only other folks who'd come down to the mouth of the Kasilof that morning. We weren't connected by what we'd left at home, but by what was right here. The ice floes, the inlet, the tide.

The kids dug into the pint of banana-split ice cream from the Kasilof store. Hig started to blow up the rafts to cross the river. The guys sat in the truck. Too much ice to set herring nets, but the sun glinted on the edges of the floes and the ice spun mesmerizingly in the current. No one was in any hurry to get home. They were adventurers too. I can't remember if we traded our "number of years in Alaska" badges, but these men had been in the state for a while. Longer than me. The chattiest of the three leaned out the open window, scratched his beard, and told us he hoped Alaska would run out of oil soon—so it might run out of newcomers: "We'll be back where we started. There won't be so many people then." The driver took another puff of his cigar and leaned out the window in agreement: "I want to keep our freedom of fishing. There are so many more people and everything's gotten so tight; it's going to get even more tied up."

The road that connects Kasilof to the beach connects it to Los Angeles too. To New York City. Anyone in the country could drive out here on an April morning to stare at the ice floes that bobbed and crunched and sloshed up and down the inlet with the tide. But they hadn't. The guys in the truck knew a future where they did show up was different from a future where they didn't.

The next river mouth once went by the Dena'ina name *Shk'ituk't*, meaning "where we slide down." So we slid down. The banks of the Kenai River slid down into calf-deep muck, and us with them, until I perched on an ice floe by a forest of pilings. Wind filled the orange inflation bag, and I squeezed its air into the raft. Lituya squirmed sleepily on my shoulder. My coat and the raft were red beneath their mud-streaks, but everything else was brushed in the cold gray wash of breakup. A propped-up fishing boat, an old cannery, gulls and eagles that shrieked and circled in the wind. Ice floes plowed into an industrial dock, crunching into shards and exploding into waves of brown ripples.

The Russians had renamed the Kenai after a different Dena'ina word that meant something like "flat" or "meadow," but there were already more than a thousand people here when they showed up, perhaps a fifth of Cook Inlet's population. People had been there for thousands of years already, parked in just the right place to receive the hordes of fish. Teeming salmon, invisible in that silt-brown glacial rush.

The record king (once people were measuring) was ninety-seven and a quarter pounds. Once the kings pass by, nearly two million sockeye stream toward Skilak Lake. But the real wealth for the Dena'ina was at the end of the season. The late-run silvers. North of here, the ground's too frozen to dig. South of here, it's too warm. But here, a pit dug into the ground is like baby bear's bowl of porridge: not too cold, not too warm—just right. Dried fish from the end of the season could be buried in the fall, frozen all winter to feed the village. When the Dena'ina figured that out, they settled down here for good. One winter day's ration was a chunk of dried fish the length of an out-stretched palm.

We crossed the Kenai River, scrambled up into an empty park where signs greeted us with a dozen different "Nos": camping, littering, parking, strewing the sand with salmon guts. In summer, the salmon come in hordes, with silver backs flashing and bellies full of eggs. A thrashing desperate journey until they're swept up into the mesh of a long-handled net to ride back to Anchorage in a cooler, in a truck behind a truck behind a truck behind a truck—each one bristling with the handles of dipnets.

The salmon often get smoked, usually get frozen, and still feed folks through the winter, come February when someone in Anchorage or Iowa might pull a vacuum-sealed package out of the chest freezer to thaw for dinner. Most Alaskans, Native or not, have one of these large white coffins out in the garage or in the arctic entry, and they sure are easier than hollowing out a pit with stone-bladed tools. It's easier to buy nets than to weave them from natural fibers. Easier to drive down the highway than to build your own boat and paddle down. The Kenai's salmon feed more people now than they ever did. Hordes come here in the summer, shoulder to shoulder with their nets or rods, squeezing each other out and squeezing out a few of Kenai's winter residents who can't even stand to stay in town for the spectacle. When the Russians showed up, there were three thousand Dena'ina in the whole Cook Inlet basin, and only about eighty thousand people in all of Alaska. Between the dipnetters on the beach and the anglers up river, 128,000 people fished on the Kenai River in 2012.

Maybe they would come even without the fish. The summer's rush of outsiders seems like as much a part of the state as the summer's rush of salmon, and the growing population seems just as inevitable. This broad flat chunk of the Kenai Peninsula had been talked up by even the very first colonists. Most of their optimistic predictions crashed into the dust, but nothing could stem the tide of newcomers. The fur trade would be an inexhaustible source of wealth, giving the Russians something to rival the Spaniards' gold and silver. But by the time they sold the territory to the Americans in 1867, nearly the only profitable business they had left was selling Kodiak Island ice to California.

Cook Inlet's coal would power the world. But not even one major mine was ever dug. Its gold would make the inlet the greatest mineral region there was, but the gold rush lasted only a few years. The Kenai Peninsula would make a "lordly cattle ranch," where the beef would be fed on a luxuriant crop of red-top hay. That never happened either. Yet people kept coming.

We scraped our boats up onto shore between the Kenai River ice floes in April—which is still mostly winter around here—because we shied away from summer's crowds. We worried we'd be squeezed out, that we'd never find room between the fishermen and the tourists.

It's a squeezed-out sort of place, this shore. The shrubs squeezed out the wispy fluffs of colonizer plants that grew on the heels of the glaciers, and the forests squeezed out the shrubs. Maybe the Dena'ina had squeezed out the ancient Riverine Kachemak people back in 1000 AD, but it's hard to know just what happened back then. Then the Russians showed up and squeezed out the sea otters, and they tried to squeeze out the Dena'ina too. The Dena'ina pushed back, however. In 1797 they ousted the handful of Russians from the fort here at the Kenai River where Captain Vancouver had found them a few years earlier, crouched behind a twelve-foot fence. Just three dozen Russian men with a dozen muskets and two brass guns, and Vancouver had scoffed at them. He thought them as unprotected as they were uncivilized, dirty and uncouth, eating cold boiled halibut between slabs of raw dried salmon. Civilized people would have bread.

The Dena'ina fought the Russians in Tyonek, in Lake Iliamna, and Kenai. And they won. Because of that, the Russians built their capital in Sitka, six hundred miles away. But smallpox and flu proved harder to overthrow. And people kept coming. The Russians. The Americans. The canneries. Commercial fishermen, subsistence fishermen, and fishermen driven by the thrill of the catch. The homesteaders and the military, the highway and the oil fields. Each group partially, but not completely, squeezing out the ones before to make room for themselves.

The ocean seemed to be working to squeeze out the people who lived here as well. Small chunks of layer-cake silt toppled from the bluffs. A gurgling sort of splash at high tide. A muffled thud onto sand. Sometimes walls rose along the shore—fortifications to battle the sea. There were the standard bulwarks of stacked cinderblocks and cobbles caged in wire mesh. Driftwood propped up in old tires. A zigzag wall built log-cabin style, focusing waves to the inside corners. An armor of sheet metal, hammered flat from an old fuel tank, the words "Jet A" still visible against the rust. A barge, disassembled into steel walls, leaning back against driftwood poles. One homeowner had simply stacked a pile of fresh spruce branches on the beach.

An ice shelf crushed against the edge of the slope, hugging walls and pilings in a dingy embrace. A rubble of concrete and twisted metal formed a jungle gym on the sand, long since dismembered from whatever house or wall it once belonged to. Katmai whacked the old pipes with a stick. They rang like a set of bells. Hig ran ahead to write words in the sand, coaxing Katmai along with sandy renditions of "cat" or "rainbow" or "wind."

We followed a rope up, hand-over-hand as our scrambling feet eroded the sand out from under us. I tried to brush it off, but it was hopeless. The engineer who'd invited us to his home said that the bluff had sloughed off more than fifteen feet last fall, and I'd brought nearly half that much back up with me, in a sandy pile of coats and boots and packs in a corner of the garage. The kids fanned out, scouring the place for new toys to play with. Above our sprawl of gear, boxes and bins reached to the garage ceiling, labeled neatly: "adult winter hats," "kid ice skates." Kayaks and skis and a bike trailer hung in their designated places, beside a Prius that was cleaner than we were. They had two kids and a massive ropes course in the backyard, and gear for every outdoor activity you could do here. They were adventurers too.

The people we met along this stretch of the highway measured the year like we do at home, watching which mountain the sun sets behind as the year creeps forward. They watch the ice floes spin past, duck-shaped, mushroom-shaped, walrus-shaped. They mush dogs and catch fish and paddle kayaks and hunt moose and burn firewood, and the fact that their world is turning more and more crowded and urban is like the fact that their bluffs are sliding piece by piece into the sea—something everyone knows and no one bothers much about, most of the time.

The engineer had actually calculated the average retreat rate he could expect at his own house. Based on the slope, the house and garage should outlast him and his wife. And the kids, with their pile of math trophies, might be somewhere else by then. Or not. Alaska's an adventurous place. It's different up here and we love it that way, even as each one of us who comes up and loves it makes the myth just a little less true. "I think," he said, "that there's a value Alaska provides to the Lower 48 in being a frontier. That people, even though most of them never will move here, have the idea that there's this place full of moose and spruce trees and salmon and they *could* move here. It gives them hope."

But what if they *do* move here? What if they *don't*? The tension of Alaskan isolationism dates back to the earliest newspaper articles, which alternated between grim assessments and optimistic boosterism, with unclear motives on both ends. One coal miner in 1888 wrote: "I hear the Alaska Commercial Company and the cannery men talking down that country . . . but I think they don't want outsiders to go in. They want to hold the country for themselves." There have always been those who think Alaska depends on bringing in folks who can plumb its riches, and people who think it depends on keeping them out.

"Before oil," a pilot told us, "this was just a wide spot in the road with a couple of homesteads. There weren't that many people here and they didn't do much." It was an adventure for anyone to get here, when homesteading opened in 1947. We met a woman who'd first flown over her hundred acres in a tiny plane, then had to hike sixty-five miles to get to her parcel from the end of the jeep trail. Her old homestead in the scraggly spruce forest now butted up against the roar of traffic and the strip malls lining the highway. To the pilot, Jim, that roar was the sound of a working economy—the sound of progress.

He spread out his maps on the table—topography I recognized, overprinted by the purple circles and radiating lines that must have meant something to an aviator. We squinted at the curves, inventing potential routes down Cook Inlet's wild western shore. I love talking to pilots. They have the same hunger for country that I do, flying over so many more miles than almost anyone sees, picking out the specks of bears in grass, imagining the textures down below.

Jim flies for the oil industry, and he'd offered to do us a favor by ferrying a box of food to one of the oil camps across the inlet, a long ways from where a road can reach. He lives on the highway, but his job depends on the fact that the highway still misses most of Alaska. Flying country is adventure country. It can be that way, for the pilots and for us, because most of Alaska still doesn't look much like the parts that people live in.

A few miles up the coast in Nikiski, a few miles south of the oil docks that thrust out into the narrowing middle of Cook Inlet, a brown bulldog stood in a doorway, framed against a baby blue sky. "He likes to sit there and look down when they're fishing," Dean said. A second bulldog nosed in beside the first, sniffing at the two-hundred-foot drop-off to the beach below. I walked over, stopped five paces back from the dogs to snap a picture, then crept just close enough to shut the door firmly. We'd shuffled house to house to house along the highway, and I'd tried to connect with each successive person on the place they loved the most—on the quirky individuality of their own adventures. But this room, hanging over a literal cliff, was the most adventurous living room I'd ever seen.

Dean had a neat plaid shirt tucked into a pair of belted jeans, and his white-gray hair frizzed out in a mane around his balding head. He offered me a cup of orange juice. Lituya crawled into my lap and grabbed the glass for herself. There was sky under both of us. On an adventure, you march right into a world that isn't arranged or labeled to make things easy for you, squint into the distance, and puzzle out the risks on your own. If that's true, Dean and Seki could open a window, lean out, and have an adventure without ever leaving home.

"Back in '69, this place was a mansion," Seki told us. "There was a pool, a spiral staircase, a barn . . ."

"Of course, the barn's long gone now. Into the ocean. The place was condemned," Dean said. "We got it for a couple thousand dollars. I don't think the borough expected anyone to move in," he laughed. The house hangs over the cliff and despite the solid concrete, it'll fall over eventually, and Dean and Seki know that.

Seki led us into the basement, where sacks of potatoes stood in the corner and sawdust shavings littered the floor. The hall was filled with the musty scent of feathers and droppings, and a quiet chaos of thin little voices going *peep-cheep-peep-cheep* behind a low barrier. Seki plucked a single large egg from an incubator, cupping it proudly in her palm. "This is from my best one-year-old layer." We'd passed by a chalkboard in the kitchen, neatly divided into rows and columns that carefully tracked the egg yield of the birds in her breeding program. Seki wore her hair in a high ponytail. Pink flowers twined down the sleeve of her sweatshirt, and when she held out a downy chick for Lituya to stroke, her smile was contagious.

Fences and netting were strung out to the very edge of the bluff on either side of the house, where turkeys with monstrously scaly red and blue heads fluffed their feathers, and geese and chickens strutted about. Volcanoes gleamed bright and snowy across Cook Inlet. No poultry farm has ever had a better view.

"The bluff once lost sixty feet in a single storm," Dean told us.

"Are you afraid you might be in here when it falls?" I asked.

"We've talked about sleeping somewhere else for the night, when there's a big fall storm."

I was the adventurer-with-toddlers here, and I was questioning *them* about risk. It felt a little backward. "I know a social worker," Seki commented. "She says Child Protective Services has been getting calls about you guys. Don't worry, though." She gave me a reassuring smile. "They don't think you're doing anything wrong." She gestured out the window. "Not in Alaska anyway."

Folks are different up here. I clung to that. It was a comfort to me, and not just because I hoped not to get a call from a misguided social worker. Wasn't Alaska full of fishing families, and hunting and snow-machining families, and other families who take their kids out to places that most Americans couldn't even imagine? It was a comfort to me, because I knew our life was different, but I still didn't want to feel alone.

I climbed up on the window seat by the dining room table, by the single pair of binoculars that was the only thing on it, and gestured the kids to come out for one last look over the edge. Adventure is different and difficult and can thrust you into an uncomfortable unknown. But it's a mistake to think that it's always risky. This wasn't risky. Even our whole eight-hundred-mile expedition wasn't risky.

Risk belongs to a moment. The bluffs along the Kenai Peninsula coast are eroding, the way that bluffs do. In a punctuated rhythm—a little bit every year, interspersed with occasional huge slides that vary in location and extent. One fall rainstorm, this house will tumble all the way down, washed into the ocean like its neighbors. Each property here slowly squeezed between the highway and the sea, until even the highway itself is squeezed out. One day. One storm. But not on this sunny spring afternoon. They have years ahead, most likely, to breed chickens and eat fried eggs at a table overhanging that sweeping view of ocean and sky, and who's to say it isn't worth it?

Risk belongs to a moment. With two toddlers in tow, we were traveling eight hundred miles through a wilderness that included blizzards and ocean and quicksand and bears. When some people read all that in the newspaper, they called CPS. But risk belongs to a moment. Not the seventy-zillionth hour of walking on sand with the weight of the two-year-old biting into your shoulders and the prattling of the four-year-old filling your ears. Not to the moment when you pretend to eat the toddler's twenty-seventh sand-and-mud pancake, or when you bite down on the real sand mixed into your rice, or when you listen to the rain thrum against the walls of the tent and wonder whether to get out of bed after all.

As that highway keeps thrumming with people, I hope it leaves room for Dean and Seki, and me, and the vegetarians feeding their dog team on fish, and the fishermen who dabble in open-source computer software, and the teacher eating dinner beneath the mounted head of a mountain goat. I hope Alaskans in the future are as weird as we are today. I hope we save room for all our adventurers. I'd rather not be squeezed out.

A slough winds through the silt flats and quicksand of Chickaloon Bay.

IN THE QUICKSAND

MAY 1-10: NIKISKI TO TURNAGAIN ARM

Current bent waves around the sharp corner of the East Forelands. The other side of Cook Inlet seemed so close here, we could almost taste it. A few miles north of the Nikiski oil docks, the houses and bluffs gave way to a backdrop of woods—a lighthouse reserve. This was the narrow spot. Only about ten miles to Kustatan on Cook Inlet's west side, but more than two hundred miles the way we were going. Who would walk all the way around to Anchorage rather than risk that paddle? Only us moderns. The Dena'ina paddled it all the time, and maybe more than one terrified Russian got toted along in the middle seat of a bidarka, wondering how the boat would thread those currents. Silt and fish rushed through that gap.

Whales opened their mouths beneath the waves. We watched them slowly push against the current, the round white backs of the adults followed by the round gray backs of the babies. Belugas. They posed between us and the oil rigs. They strung out in ones and twos and threes, and seemed to pass us constantly, until I wondered if there were dozens of whales or just the same small handful, circling in an endless loop to feed in the riches of the fastest water.

The yolks from Dean and Seki's eggs were wobbly and yellow-orange on the instant mashed potatoes—totally worth carrying this far beyond their precarious poultry farm. We were alone now. The road had pulled away from the coast, tracing a more direct path to Anchorage. March had turned to April, then to May, and we'd cast our lot with the anticipation of spring. The double-walled tent, the wood stove, my rubber boots—I'd mailed home every scrap of winter gear, and the silt rushed in through the mesh on my running shoes. Our summer tent was a damper, smaller version of the winter one we'd sent home, and the third of May was only a damp, small version of summer. It had been a long time since we'd slept in this tent—had we ever even seam-sealed it? Occasional drips hung from the plastic clips along the interior seams, and I fastened a Ziploc bag to each to catch the water. I balled up my raincoat as a pillow.

My cheeks, in the morning, were stubbled with sand. *Thwack!* I whipped the wet sock at the least-sandy side of my backpack. *Thwack! Thwack! Thwack!* Two limp navy blue socks, followed by two small and crumpled gray socks, followed by two even tinier blue ones. Wring, *thwack,* brush off the rest, carefully wiggle onto each appropriate foot.

The kids piled on my lap as I snapped and tied and zipped their clothes around them. The snow crept almost down to the edge of the sand, and just outside, steam puffed from the pot of hot water, from Hig's breath, and from the drying ring of sand around the fire. "Want to eat by the fire?" They did. We were all drawn to the flame, but I held myself back to pack up, shaking and stuffing each fleece shirt, each granola bar, each diaper pad. Katmai balanced on a sandy log, embracing the cold and gritty world. There was nothing to linger for in the tent. Our fires were outdoors now.

It had been a week of urban travel from Kasilof through Nikiski, and we'd wound our sandy trail through more spare rooms and basements than I could picture, sweeping behind every footstep. The beauty of the great outdoors is that it is *already* messy. Sweeping? Scrubbing? The floor is sand! The kids can scatter dirt all over the beach, and no one minds if they break the driftwood toys. Our possessions are strewn in garish obviousness across the gray and brown. No plugged-in chargers to remember to pull, no messages, no names or errands to crowd my mind. Arctic terns swooped and keened above the inlet, and from the bushes a bird I couldn't name cried, "I'm ready! I'm ready! I'm ready!" One more diaper and we'd be ready too.

Blocks of granite rose from craters of mud. Five feet tall, ten feet, twenty. Boulder after boulder, thrown down on the shore, in the tide flats, out into the inlet until the water curled around their blocky edges and the lines of rocks blurred into nothing in the fog. You could imagine setting a tent on the flatter ones. You could imagine some god of the sky throwing down a handful of pebbles, or a mythical creature bounding the many yard gaps from rock to rock. Stepping stones of giants.

Rivers carry sand and pebbles. Glaciers carry whatever they want. Person-sized, house-sized, the rocks had been only a smudge on the ice that filled Cook Inlet. They flowed with the ice and fell, erratically, wherever they happened to be when the ice melted out from underneath them. Hig set his next fire right on top of one of these glacial erratics and shooed the kids away. "Don't topple the fire!"

"It's precarious!" Katmai screeched, tugging at Lituya's arm. She collapsed onto him with a yelp, and he shoved her away.

I ducked under the edge of a chunk of granite, calling sweetly, "Did you see this cave? It's *huge!*" Huge enough, at least, to distract a squabble. Boulders leaned together to form a rubble of caves and arches. Drips fell like a curtain at the entrance to the cave. They rippled the bird-bath puddles on the top of the boulders. Lituya stretched out on her belly as she climbed, splashing elbow-deep into each and every pool until the fire finally out-sputtered the rain and lunch was ready.

"Lituya's a Not-follow-the-rules-a-saurus!" Katmai's voice wavered between laughter and serious elder brother admonishment.

She leapt onto Hig's back, again. Hig set her down gently, again. "You just can't climb on me when I'm sewing by the fire," he explained, his voice steady as ever, despite his rising impatience. "And the M&Ms are put away now." Lituya wrinkled her face into a grumpy knot and tossed her lunch into the fire, before stomping with all thirty pounds of two-year-old fury on every piece of gear she could reach. She was tired now as well as soaked. I picked her up, and her sandy eyelids scrunched closed against the raindrops as she tried to fall asleep on my back.

The gray sky bounced off the puddles, and rivulets of rich brown wandered down the beach, setting off the rough edges of the erratics. Hours later, the rain stopped. The tide and fog retreated together, multiplying the lines of boulders. Hig and I each stretched down to clutch the hand of a child, leaving quivering footprints in the tide flats as we headed out to climb the rocks. We weren't even dry yet. Still gritty and half-chilled, we were more relaxed than we'd ever been in town. It was just the four of us again, and it felt perfect.

We journey to explore the country. To meet people, to ask questions, to scratch an inexplicable itch for adventure. We journey because it's the best way I've ever found to be a family.

We journey by foot, or by sea. In and out of the boats, back and forth between water and land, every day that the wind and waves allowed. The tide pulsed up the inlet, and we followed it, paddling when it swelled our direction. I flicked the paddle, turned the packraft into a narrow gap between two boulders, and ground to a halt. My butt—the most laden and lowest-hanging part of the packraft—scraped up onto a boulder that hunched, invisible, just below the surface. "Oops!" Katmai laughed as he and Hig passed me, and I wriggled myself back into the water.

The same airy lightness that makes a packraft seem so vulnerable also makes it tough. Paddle as hard as you can toward any obstacle—a rock, an iceberg, the shore—and watch yourself get flung right back again like an underweight bumper car. Captain Vancouver despaired of avoiding the erratics, which encumbered the whole space with "an immense number of conical rocks, detached from each other, in a bank of sand and small stones that extended a league and upwards from shore."

Vancouver never hit a rock. Cook didn't either, but both of them grounded on sandbars in the middle of the inlet and were lucky to escape so easily. Where there aren't boulders, there are sandbars or reefs. The history of Alaskan shipping is full of boats hitting things they thought they could avoid, all the way up to the *Exxon Valdez* tanker and even more modern wrecks. People look at our little rafts and they think we're crazy, but sometimes being slow and small is the safest thing out there.

Captain Cook didn't even mention the rocks. His ships were pushed and pulled, stalled and swept by the currents that rocked the inlet. Just a few days to spend in the inlet that would later bear his name, and he filled the log with his notes on the fresh taste of the water at a dropping tide, the swirling brown, the remains of trees crashed about in the currents. This place was a river, he was certain, and best to find the proof quickly and be done with it all. It was the first of June, and "the delay thus occasioned was an essential loss. The season was advancing apace." So he sent his boats up into Knik Arm, into Turnagain, observing the height of the land, distinguishing islands from shores, convincing all who would come after that this was no Northwest Passage.

But first, he sent the second officer ashore with two armed boats and a flag. A bottle. A few English coins minted in 1772. As Lieutenant King pulled ashore, twenty Dena'ina men and their dogs approached the foreigners, gesturing for them to drop their muskets. Cook's men dropped their guns. They buried the bottle. They brandished their flag with incomprehensible words. Then the ship's surgeon bought a dog, picked up his musket, and shot it dead. The twenty men watching quickly scrambled their own weapons from the bushes behind them—poised and ready—surely tense and confused. The foreigners left. The bottle the men had buried contained a piece of paper, inscribed with the ship names and the date. Plenty sufficient, in their minds, to own a piece of the world. Meanwhile, Cook busied the rest of the crew in getting the ships under sail.

On the chart it was inked in as Point Possession, and that was as much possession as they were inclined to bother with. Cook, and in his opinion, Great Britain, wanted none of this swampy ground, this poor black soil, this shrubby distant land where even on the first of June, they saw not a single plant in flower. With the exception of the sea otter, even the furs offered up for trade seemed to him poor, sparse, made into worn-out clothing. But perhaps the Natives simply had no reason to hunt more? Cook mused that more trade with foreigners would surely introduce the Natives to new luxuries, increasing their wants until they were much more assiduous in procuring a plentiful supply of skins. Perhaps the inlet itself could be useful in trade or settlement. "If the discovery of this great river," he wrote, "which promises to vie with the most considerable ones already known to be capable of extensive inland navigation, should prove of use either to the present, or to any future age, the time we spent in it ought to be the less regretted." Perhaps Cook just wanted to feel that his mission wasn't a failure.

"People come looking for it, you know." The woman riding on the four-wheeler told us: "Cook's bottle." They'd stopped on the beach to talk to us, a middle-aged couple on a single machine, towing a trailer behind them. They wore matching boxy black coats over camo pants, and she pushed up her goggles onto her pink fuzzy hood. Rummaging in the trailer, she found a bag of jumbo-sized marshmallows for the kids. She'd just retired from working in the oilfields of Alaska's North Slope. This was the couple's first spring visit to the setnet site at Point Possession; they needed to prep for the summer season. This site was her home, and her parents' home, and their parents' home, and so on. "My family's been here for a thousand years," she explained. "My ancestors met Cook's ships. Now people come looking for his bottle, and no one's ever found it. Of course they haven't. I've always thought that my ancestors must have been watching them from just behind the bushes. I think they dug up that bottle just as soon as Cook's men left."

Point Possession juts north to form the entrance to Turnagain Arm. Hig and I ran around the corner it makes— all puffed up with clothes and suddenly sweaty to match pace with Katmai's enthusiastic sprint. We ran until the boulders fell away, until the land and trees turned to march south again, and the way we were going was blocked by the looming distance of Chickaloon Bay. It seemed a placid, calm, lake-like thing. Fourteen miles end to end, but the tidal currents should surely help us across.

My paddle shafts scratched against the raft tube, rolling gritty brown water back and forth against the plastic. We were miles from shore, and the only ones out here with us were a few seagulls perched on muddy ice pans, lazily flapping away as we passed. "There's got to be a channel here somewhere." I stared uselessly into the brown, then back up at the distant mountains on the other side of the arm. If I stopped paddling, let the raft's momentum still and squinted carefully at the peaks, was that near mountain moving past the far one?

Hig, in the other raft, was performing the same dead reckoning. "No noticeable current here. I think we must be over the shallows. Maybe there's a channel farther out?"

"We're already a long way from shore." Navigation in a big empty bay is difficult—channels and currents are hard to read, distance is challenging to guess, and of course we'd never been here before. The wind began to blow. Cold, from the north. The current began to pick up. Also from the north. We paddled this way and that, but all the channels were the same. All pointed inland. Chickaloon Bay was a vast gaping mouth, swallowing the gull-speckled ice pans, swallowing us, swallowing everything. My paddle stroke stuttered. Each blade hit the mud with a solid thump. The ice pans grounded and stopped. We shoved the rafts between them, where the waves focused and broke in the few inches of water, slopping their muddy curls over the sides of the packrafts. Arctic terns leapt from the floes, wheeling and keening overhead. Lituya popped awake, a muddy splash on her left cheek. "Where are we?"

"Aground."

In 1895 the steamship *Elwood* sat right where we were, aground on the mud in Chickaloon Bay, three miles from the channel and sucked in, like we were, by the sudden fall of the tide. Another steamship passed it by, penning a breezy note about the grounding it would carry to a Seattle newspaper: "There was no danger at all, as the passengers could walk ashore, and were practically at their destination." These passengers were miners, heading for the gold fields of Turnagain Arm, and they must have clambered off the boat with the same chilly squelch, crunch, squelch, crunch that we did, headed the same direction. Squelch, crunch, squelch, crunch, mud, ice. Cold. A gooey ice bath swirling through our socks as we held Katmai by the hands, swinging him across the deepest sloughs to find the nearest solid land to pitch a tent on.

But what was mud, when there was gold at stake? What is cold, when adventure surrounds you?

The tide was low again the next morning, as we squelched our way back toward where Chickaloon mud turned into Chickaloon Bay. But it was rising. We hoped to paddle, and we pulled our rafts behind us like dirty rubber ducklings. Hig's footprints formed a line of water-filled holes ahead of me, run over by the packraft's slithering drag mark. Katmai's smaller footprints formed water-filled holes behind me, and his muddy face twitched into a scowl. "I can't walk here!"

In that moment, I couldn't either. I'd been walking on tiptoes—the better to keep my sneakers attached to my feet. Then, suddenly, the mud rose up, and I dropped down. It slipped and pooled around my ankles, blobbing slowly upward until it stopped, leaving me balanced like an awkwardly encased ballerina, pointed toes set into the just-over-knee-deep goo.

Up ahead, Hig yelled something I couldn't quite make out. "I can't hear you!" I yelled back. "Bring back the packraft!"

"I want to catch up to Dad!" Katmai yelled. "Help me out of the mud!"

"Wait a minute. Don't pull your feet out. Just wait. Or . . ." Did he have the thirty seconds of patience required? "Or lie down." Lying down would work, but Hig was just right there, tugging the packrafts back to us along the deep liquid tracks he'd set before. *Shlooop, shloop, shloop.* I waved him over, my lower body poised like a statue in the quicksand. You don't sink if you don't struggle. *Shlooop, shloop, shloop,* and I flopped onto the packraft, throwing all my weight onto that bouncy cushion of air like it was a life ring. It floated me. My legs popped free of the mud with a satisfying *shlllllluuuuuuuuuck!*

"Me too! Me too!" Katmai was too light to sink in—not even to his knees, which hovered a muddy inch or two above the ground. A simple handhold would have sufficed to pull him free, but my way looked like too much fun, and he flopped onto the packraft too. "Can you pull me in the raft?" he asked, wiggling his muddy feet against the sides.

"The tide is coming," said Hig. "I think we can paddle now." Water rushed in as we paddled away. It crept up to the very top of the dunes, pouring over the peaks and ridges, turning the quicksand back into a bay. Somewhere under there, my footprints were buried, filling with silt as quickly as they'd sunk down beneath me, the water rising far above where my head had been. But I wasn't buried.

Our scheme had worked. We had escaped the quicksand. Quicksand is Indiana Jones–type stuff. Hissing snakes, a swinging pendulum that might chop your head off, and a dramatic chase through mystical desert ruins. As a kid I'd thought it was just as fictional. Sand and silt are carried by water, and in most places you've ever seen, they're set down again in a sedate and orderly fashion, as the water sweeps away. Voilà, a beach! But nothing happens instantly. Each piece of sand takes a little bit of time to make its way from the top of the water to the bottom.

Glacial silt, which makes up most of the shores of Upper Cook Inlet—the thing that turns all this water thick and brown—is smaller than sand. It takes longer to fall. The silt is locked in a race with the tide. The tide is monstrous, pulling faster and faster, sucking the flats dry, and the silt just doesn't have time to settle. It doesn't compact. Grains don't stack against other grains, and the shining flats that stretch before you aren't really beaches at all. The low spots are filled with a quivering soup of silt suspended in the water that couldn't make it out in time.

Quicksand is a killer. One time, back in the 1960s, a man stuck in the Turnagain Arm quicksand was torn in half by a helicopter trying to pull him out. At least, that's what people say. The truth is worse. The would-be rescuers had him hold the barrel of his rifle as a breathing tube while the tide swept over him, until it slipped from his hypothermia-weakened hands and he died beneath the icy rising tide. The helicopter tried to pull the body later. It was the helicopter's cable that snapped.

In another grisly instance, a young couple had tried to drive across the Arm on four-wheelers in the 1980s. The machine got stuck, then she got stuck when she tried to push it out. Her husband freed one of her legs, but the rescuers who brought another breathing tube could do nothing to stop the tide. Quicksand only forms where the water sweeps in and out twice a day—only forms in places where the tide moves so quickly that the silt can't settle in time, where the rescuers, as well as the ground-up rock, can lose their race with the sea.

It looks solid. But a footstep does what the tide never had time to—it compacts the grains of silt. Beneath your weight, that takes only a second. Suddenly, you're sunk in what a physicist might call a non-Newtonian shear-strengthening fluid. Did you ever play with cornstarch and water as a kid? Remember the way the white soup you could dribble off a spoon solidified into a sudden jarring hardness when you slapped the surface? Imagine being buried in that. If you move through it oh-so-gently, it just might hold. But one quick move, one slap, one panicked wrenching of a stuck leg, and it hardens around you, swallowing you deeper. Modern rescuers have pumps to inject water around a victim's legs, special boots to avoid getting stuck, and many people have been freed. People live all around Turnagain Arm. But fear keeps the flats emptier than they were in the gold-mining days.

The dribbling remains of quicksand clung to my shoes, which served for several hours as Lituya's muddy pillow. Katmai named each peak that bordered the bay as we crept closer and closer to them. Blob Top. Steep Side. Cloud Reach. Chickaloon Bay swallowed the tide, but we were far enough, this time, that we were going to get past it.

"What's *that* part of the tent?" Katmai chirped.

"It's called a rain fly," our old friend Erik replied. He had come down from Anchorage to travel the rest of Turnagain Arm with us.

"This thing, this thing, what's this thing?!"

"A stove."

"Why do you have a stove?" Our children were thrilled with every bit and bobble of Erik's hiking gear, drilling him on each item as it came out of his pack, spilled out onto the lawn in the middle of town that served as Hope's public campground. We were thrilled too. Erik worked at REI and while we'd become codgerly old adventurers who just kept on walking with a new copy of whatever we'd been used to, Erik knew about the latest innovations in solar chargers and water filters—things we might need for the next phase of our journey.

It was early May, and downtown Hope was boarded up, as if the town's 192 people listed in the most recent census had rolled over in bed, peeked out at the lack of spring, and decided to keep hibernating. Only tourists milled about, strewn across the lawn that served as the public campground. The young people with the bikes and the little white car were in Alaska for an upcoming kayak-guiding job. The older couple had a tent, a trailer, and a gold dredge. Hope was supposedly named for an early prospector, but I can think of no better name for a gold rush town. Hope was what brought them here. Hope and rumors.

Rumors traveled slowly then. They were folded into letters, carried by steamships, printed in outside newspapers, which were carried back north on other steamships, which provoked another round of letters. "Cook Inlet A Delusion!" cried the *Seattle Post-Intelligencer* in October of 1895, reporting that two hundred miners were stranded and starving in Turnagain Arm, lacking even the money to get home. Those miners who'd made it out were promptly shipwrecked in Yakutat, stranded there for a weary month of fall before a mail steamer could retrieve them. But even some of the shipwrecked were plotting their trip back to the gold fields.

In December, two months after the original lambasting, Seattle finally received a scathing response signed by a slew of those Turnagain miners: "All we can say is that the boom is not petered out and that there are not 200 miners in 'far away Alaska' who are stranded. If there are, all we can say is that it is their own fault, and that next season will prove to the people outside of far away Alaska that Turnagain Arm, Cook Inlet, has some very rich placer diggings. . . . There was no need for any man to leave this camp this summer without some gold dust in his pocket."

With so little communication, even a single letter writer could shape the migration of thousands. Gold-struck hopefuls read the back-and-forth and plotted their own adventure. When spring came, they flooded north. Cook Inlet was soon eclipsed by the Klondike, but people still spilled over into Hope and the next-door town of Sunrise. In the summer of 1898, there were eight hundred people in Sunrise, and it was the biggest town in Alaska, with Hope close behind, and those numbers didn't count the prospectors camped out in the hills and the valleys.

There were eight thousand prospectors in Cook Inlet that summer, hopeful targets of the Alaska Commercial Company ads. Their steamships could get you and your mining gear there—to prospect in Cook Inlet's "balmy climate"—for the low price of fifteen dollars per ton, sailing from Seattle on the eighth of every month of summer. Newspapers printed the names of returning miners who brought home the most gold, to the tune of four thousand dollars a man. Natives boated the mail between Sunrise and Knik, and sold the miners moose meat for five cents a pound. There was a brewery to go along with Hope's pair of bars and even a school by 1904, despite the fact that almost none of the prospectors stayed the winter, and that the population purportedly consisted of "200 men, 2 white women, and 1 native woman."

Twice a day, the tide came past Hope in a roaring stampede. The waves were loud and brown and jumbled, clambering all over each other in an attempt to be first, collapsing into a chaos of curls and whirlpools. The Dena'ina called it *nudidghul*—an onomatopoetic meant to evoke the roar of the water. The tidal bore marches up Turnagain Arm like a clockwork tsunami. Surfers can ride it for miles. Back in the prospecting days, that wave snatched and sunk a sloop with nine men in it, and only the captain's dog survived. Now we sat on the beach to watch it all happen, and then it was past. Turnagain was a river, going our way. We floated it. We floated and we walked, and we played beneath the mud-daubed nests of spring's returned swallows. For all the company we had, the map of Turnagain Arm may well have said "Here There Be Dragons."

People weren't always so afraid of Turnagain. The miners had to get here somehow. There were no roads then. No tide tables telling the time to the minute, no weather predictions, no local fire departments, no hoses or helicopters. Sometimes wind rushes through the narrow gap in the mountains, meets the tide, and whips the whole thing into a frothy meringue. People crossed back and forth and picked their way around, but sometimes they couldn't. Sometimes they were stranded on Fire Island at the mouth of the Arm with a working boat. Or without one, camped out eating rabbits until someone else happened by. This used to be normal.

Standards have changed.

"How about you guys sit in the raft?" I suggested. "While we blow the other one up."

"Or play over here?" Hig added. "On the other side of us, maybe sitting down?"

"Why?" Katmai asked.

"Just for a few minutes," I dodged.

"Why?"

"So the cars won't see you," Hig explained, squeezing another bag full of air into the yellow packraft.

"Why?" Katmai was relentless.

"Because we don't want anyone to think we're in trouble." Turnagain Arm was narrow here, and it looked more like a savannah than an inlet. Dried brown grass and a handful of bushes, and we crossed three-quarters of it without seeing water at all.

Katmai picked off the seed heads of last year's grass, tossing them into the wind. "See that flight? Did you know that the ones with more seeds close together fly better? It's because they catch more air. And having less air around them outside makes them fly better."

Nevertheless, preschool science had to bend to the world's more timely demands. The tide *was* coming. I snapped paddles together while Hig and Erik blew up boats. We worked quickly. The cars zoomed past, and I couldn't imagine they would even notice us, they were going so fast. But if they did look, what would they see? Three adults and two tiny kids, standing on the far side of the channel from the road, in the middle of Turnagain

Arm, no boats in sight and the water rising? Please, no one call in a rescue.

We climbed in the boats, paddling away as the water rose over the spot where we'd been standing. It wasn't far, but each stroke was a straining battle against the wind. The rafts bounced over the small chop where the wind fought the tide, until we climbed up and over the metal highway railing next to speed limit signs and drivers who now really were staring at us. Anchorage is within spitting distance of Turnagain Arm, and the roar of the cars was like a punctuated fury that led me to clutch my kids tighter than I ever did beside the waves.

We were approaching civilization.

Viewed from the far side of Knik Arm, dwarfed by the Chugach Mountains, downtown Anchorage shimmers in the sunset.

BOOMTOWN

MAY 11–21: TURNAGAIN ARM TO ANCHORAGE

The tide drained out of Turnagain Arm on a channel that paralleled the highway. A few cars honked and waved as we passed. One woman, possibly drunk, shouted unintelligible questions about our "kayaks" from a pullout. Curious? Worried? Confused? "We're fine!" Hig yelled. "We're just heading on our way."

It was Saturday afternoon, and the fair weather brought out hooligan fishermen with buckets and nets, craned over the water to exchange a few words before the current swept us by. Hooligan—eulachon—are small fatty smelt that rush the creeks in spring before even the first of the salmon. They're so fatty that a single dried fish would burn like a candle, and their grease was traded inland for hundreds of miles.

Kids threw rocks into the inlet. Adults drove golf balls. *Thwack, whoosh, plop,* and the balls bobbled and swirled in the outgoing tide. Maybe we'd run into them again on the other side of the inlet. On the shore, there were forests—shattered white spikes drowned when the 1964 earthquake dropped the land. Nearly fifty years later, in all the winds of Turnagain, I was shocked that any were still standing. The old Girdwood gas station rots away in the tide marsh that rose around it then, as a monument to that quake. The new one—a gleaming Tesoro—was a shining beacon in the not-wilderness, full of snacks and kid-bribing ice cream.

Beyond Girdwood, a bike trail parallels the highway, which parallels the north side of Turnagain Arm. The tides flushed us down the inlet for half of each day. But for the other half of the day, the tide was against us. So half of each day, we walked. A smooth stripe of pavement rose up between moldering coffee cups and leafless brush, and Katmai was immediately over the edge. Down in the ditch with rotted leaves and napkins to fetch a tattered trash bag that had caught his eye. He tossed it into the breeze, small feet slapping on the pavement as he rushed ahead. He squealed, leapt, and tackled that bag against the ground. Then again. And again. He played with it for hours, and when he tired of chase, Hig held the bag just out of reach as Katmai jumped to catch the dangling red handles. A kid sees the possibilities in anything.

When it had space, the bike trail wound into birch and spruce and hemlock forest. Other times, it was just a stripe on the far side of the highway guardrail. The pavement pressed against the balls of my feet until I wished for just a little bit of the give of sticky mud. We chatted with weekend dog-walkers. We chatted with brightly dressed cyclists fixing a flat while Lituya peeked at the kids in their trailer. We asked anyone we could corner, "What is the future of this place, in fifty or a hundred years?" And the answers swirled around the same topics they always did. Population crowding in, oil going bust, economics and climate change, salmon and energy. The tidal bore churned up the inlet—fast and powerful; many people wondered if we could get our energy from that. There were too many to talk to all of them. Bicycle bells rung, joggers smiled, dogs turned our way with a sniff. Cars shot by. I stopped to read all the interpretive signs—passing snatches of history along to the kids. It was noisy but also calm, simple, even beautiful.

The north side of Turnagain is the highway. It's always been, for us, the last of the four- or five-hour slog from Homer to Anchorage. Even as an adult, I've thought about this area mostly as "Are we there yet?" We were smashed up against the road much more than we ever had been on the Kenai Peninsula. Here the snowy peaks plunge straight into the ocean, and in some places it's hard to even fit the highway. Block-scarred cliffs loom above the road, textured by the explosions that created them—explosions that moved a mountain from where the road should be. The season's first tourists streaked by in clean RVs and gleaming tour busses, and I imagined what it would be like to be one of them. Our grubby family just a blur on the side of the road, while they looked out on those mountains, the sky, all that grandeur they'd saved up to experience, flashing past their windows.

We got to keep on staring at this grandeur. Our way is so slow. We slept in Portage and in Girdwood, and as the gray that passed for a May evening swept over the sky, a friend of a friend recognized us and pulled over onto the shoulder of the road to offer his leftover pizza dinner. We hid our yellow-and-gray tent in the trees. Camping so close to the urban world felt a little seedy, somehow. Like something that wouldn't be allowed. We hadn't asked anyone for permission. Rain splashed the tent and poured onto the control box for the electric fence we'd set up in case of bears, and I watched sparks flash from the black knob to the red one. I turned it off. It needed glue.

The next morning, I crept out of our campsite in the woods to fill my pot from a creek that crossed the trail. Joggers streaked past in shorts and muddy trail runners. My raingear was dirty, ragged, and homemade to start with. The black pot was dented, obviously not made out of pricy titanium. I wondered if I looked like the kind of person who was homeless on purpose or by accident. A train rushed past. The railroad tracks nudged up against the highway, barely managing to share the narrow space.

In 1902 and 1903 ads for the Alaska Central Railroad were splashed across the pages of Seattle papers. Shares went for fifty dollars. Businessman John Ballaine said you couldn't lose. The route slashed through the state, a thick ribbed line on a cartoon map, with riches scrawled hopefully in all caps: gold, copper, quartz, timber, coal, fine grazing land, fine agricultural land. Thirty million dollars poured in. Trees fell, tracks were laid, tunnels were blasted before Ballaine's vision and the railroad crept north from Seward, steel on gravel on knocked-down spruce, until the locomotives puffed to the flats of shining silt. And stopped. Workers pulled their heavy boots out of the mud, dodged quicksand, and piled freight into boats. The tracks didn't make it past Girdwood. The freight rode the Turnagain tides.

We too rode the Turnagain tides, less intimidating now that we'd spent a few days in their swirls. We floated until the current turned against us, and then scrambled quickly over the guardrail and across the tracks, before the railroad maintenance crew could object. The flats were too narrow for a bike trail now, but foot trails punched up into the steep foothills above the road. We were an easy drive from Anchorage, and Erik drove down to join us again, now on the other side of Turnagain. His wife, Jenna, packed their baby for an afternoon's walk. Leafless cottonwoods crowded over our heads, the baby batted a balloon tied to the baby carrier, and I wondered why I'd never thought of a trick so clever. Dogs strained at their leashes as their owners ran past. Katmai ran and ran until he ended up stripped down to blue fleece pants and a pair of sneakers, his skin a pale blur against last fall's leaves.

The dirt was stomped flat and clear at the viewpoints, where we could drink in all of Turnagain Arm in one huge gulp. I could see the shimmering quicksand of Chickaloon Bay, and the island we'd scrambled up on when we'd finally escaped it. I could see Hope. I could see the ghost town of Sunrise, its name a twist on the gloomy darkness of that north-facing valley. The sun would rise three times a day there, popping into the gaps between the mountains for three brief flashes of daylight.

The view was almost dizzying. You forget, after a month and a half of a water's-eye view, what looking down even feels like. We were almost always on the beach or in the water that washed up against it. Late March had slid into the middle of May, and we'd passed by hundreds of miles of shore. I hadn't counted exactly, but Anchorage was somewhere close to halfway. We were going around Cook Inlet. But we'd cut across the head of Kachemak Bay and several of its fjords. We'd cut across the head of Turnagain Arm, and more shortcuts loomed ahead of us. Walking every wave-lapped boulder would make the trip a thousand miles—or infinite. "Around" was not exact. Our route along the coast was not exact. We walked on trails—roads occasionally—as well as on the sand. But we tried to stick close to the shore.

The inlet itself was the framework this place grew on. People settled down by the ocean. The ocean brought the salmon and the seals. The ocean had brought the Russians, the explorers, the prospectors, and everything else that washed up from the outside world like a line of kelp and driftwood. The road was a stubby afterthought, only a bit over two hundred miles compared to the eight-hundred-mile edge we were walking. The road brought people, but even in this populated, most central part of Alaska, roadless is the default state. I was eager to return to it. The road was noisy and dangerous. It stank of trucks in ill-repair, and what if my kids dashed out onto it? Anchorage loomed a day ahead, and it already seemed interminable.

"These live in my grass home," Lituya declared, clutching her twigs.

"What do they eat?" Katmai asked.

"They eat . . . leaves."

"Do they have any defense?"

"They eat leaves, and with their big teeth," she answered.

"I think they're camouflaged to the dirt," Katmai offered. Each kid wiggled a handful of anthropomorphized sticks, while I tried to find a handful of generic sticks for the fire.

"I think we can get to the first house pretty easily tomorrow," Hig said, studying the map. Katmai wanted to make it *today*, but it was miles ahead still. I puzzled over the map of Anchorage, plotting our assault on the city as if it were a swath of ocean cut through by a necklace of tiny islands. Each island was the home of someone who had agreed to host us. The rest of the distance was a crush of roads and fences and concrete—utterly uncampable.

Katmai was tired, and Lituya wasn't napping. He crouched on every manhole cover like a fastidious city inspector, nose almost on the metal, tracing the letters with a finger, wrenching on my hand as I tried to tug him forward. We read off the numbers on the mailboxes. House number 16860 . . . 16750 . . . "Where are we going Mama?"

"To number 16040."

"Will it be soon?" he whined.

"I don't know." It wasn't the best of days. Anchorage sprawled out before us, a dozen more miles of streets between us and the point where downtown thrust toward the narrowest part of Knik Arm.

Anchorage is not an anchorage. It's a snub-nosed triangle of land jutting out into the mudflats of Cook Inlet, dividing its headwaters into Knik and Turnagain arms. It's surrounded by shallow mudflats, swept by powerful currents, and piled, in the winter, with slushy pans of moving ice. No one ever thought it was a good place to anchor boats, but it seemed like a good place for trains.

By 1910 the gold rush was over. The towns of Hope and Sunrise had lost their luster, now barely a blip in the census. Salmon canneries were the boom of the day, and six thousand people came to Alaska in the summer to work them. Some stayed all year. Non-natives became more numerous than Natives in the Alaska census. Five-sixths of those newcomers were male. Half of them were foreigners—Scandinavians mostly—and all were foreign to Alaska. They were still just dots in the wilderness. Around Cook Inlet, an average town had a hundred or a couple of hundred residents. Hunting, fishing, maybe growing a few potatoes, selling salmon to the canneries and pelts to the trading posts.

In the early 1900s, Americans believed in the power of railroads. People had heard the miners' stories—seen photos of gear dragged through snowy passes—and wondered what riches might come if that were made easy. If Ballaine couldn't do it, the government would. President Woodrow Wilson stepped in. Cordova was a better port than Seward. Extending that town's Copper River railway would be the cheapest move. But the president's newly appointed commission knew better than to buy a rail line owned by the unpopular Guggenheims. The route would be Seward to Fairbanks. Halfway between these endpoints, Anchorage was born.

By 1915 there were two thousand people at Ship Creek, in canvas wall tents facing each other across the rutted swaths of mud that passed for streets. Just offshore of the creek mouth was the "Knik Anchorage," where steamships paused while ferrying supplies and passengers to the nearby village of Knik. Then an enterprising soul took the steamship *Bertha,* dry-docked it on one of those rutted streets, and built it into a department store called "The Anchorage." The name settled over the brand-new town, almost by accident. Residents campaigned to rename it Alaska City, but the post office refused to switch.

It became Alaska's city anyway. Why? It could have become another boom-and-bust town like any of the gold towns. Could have dwindled to the zero that was Sunrise. But Anchorage had at least a little more sun and flat ground to build on. Twenty years after that feverish founding, Anchorage was puttering along at nearly the same couple thousand people it started out with. The railroad hadn't yet had a profitable year. Anchorage was big for Alaska, but nothing anyone might recognize as a city. That took another act of government.

By the late 1930s, the world was falling toward war. Alaska was a dangling bit of unprotected territory—an unused lookout. Something had to be done. In 1940, Fort Richardson was built in Anchorage. In 1942 the Army Corps of Engineers set its soldiers on seven months of fever-pitched construction through Canada's boreal forest. The Alcan highway was the first land connection between Alaska and the Lower 48. Then, fifteen hundred miles from Anchorage, the Japanese invaded Attu and Kiska islands in the Aleutian chain. Alaska was flooded with soldiers. By 1943 there were 152,000 of them. They made up 60 percent of the territory's population. Soldiers needed housing. Soldiers needed food. Soldiers needed roads.

The war machine built Anchorage as its base, and when World War II ended, the Cold War heated up. The war machine powered the state's economy for thirty years, cementing Anchorage's reign. The biggest city in Alaska, Anchorage is now home to over three hundred thousand people—nearly half the state's population. The maps we carried, USGS topographic maps, were another great effort spurred by that war, and the Anchorage they showed was a thin spidering of roads through vast swaths of green long since turned to concrete.

We left our first Anchorage house in a crash. Toys were thrown. There was the incident of jam-smeared-in-hair, in which the elder brother claimed no responsibility in egging his sister on. Then there was the incident of the broken-wing-of-the-irreplaceable-handmade-clay-angel, and finally (this took them exactly one minute while I desperately hurried to move our bags outside) the incident of pulling out every single drawer in the bedroom dresser until the whole thing toppled, scattering its contents far and wide. No one was hurt. Give it ten more minutes, though, and maybe the whole house would go up in flames. We left the scene with more apologies, in as much haste as your average set of burglars.

Town is more stressful than wilderness. Or perhaps my particular offspring were about as well suited to civilization as a pair of rowdy bear cubs. A child might frame it like this: On a wilderness day, you wake up when you wake up. Your parents are there, starting the fire, making you breakfast, helping you with your clothes. They may talk to each other—route planning at the very least—but manage to fit every word in the spaces between your needs. They seamlessly toss off sentences like this: "I think we should . . . (your dinosaur is next to your sleeping bag) . . . walk to this point first . . . (on the other side of your sleeping bag) . . . and then . . . (let me zip up your coat) . . . start paddling . . . (here's a granola bar) . . . because the tide . . . (okay, I unwrapped it) . . . is high at 10:45." You throw mud, if you feel like it. Stomp on sticks, peer into the spaces between the stones. If you manage to break one, you can show it off with pride.

But on a town day, you stay up late and wake up early. Stay out of the way while your parents pack—because they're scrubbing and sweeping just behind your footsteps. Don't touch that! Or that! The adults are meeting other adults. And now other adults. Pose for a picture. Now be quiet, they're talking about grownup stuff. Don't squeeze the ketchup on the restaurant table. Now you don't even get ketchup to play with. The walk is just as long, but the yards are not available for playing in. They hold your hand too tight as those cars rush by. Why not just pee right here? What's so different about this bush than the ones on the beach? Who *wouldn't* whine at all that?

"Are you the McKittricks?" The man crossed the street, wiped his hands on his greasy jeans, and then decided not to offer a handshake. "I've been working on my transmission," he explained. "I'm a big fan of your book, and your website." It was the second time in a couple of days we'd been recognized by strangers. Our nondescript thirty-something faces didn't stick out too much. Our paddles did stick out—bristling from Hig's pack, with dangling life vests to match. Two adults, two kids, equipped for a stormy ocean on a residential street—that stuck out. His name was Travis. We told him (with all the appropriate caveats) all about how fun it could be to adventure in Turnagain Arm.

Recognition was our fault. We were on our way to meet a reporter on a street corner a few miles away. We had a date on a radio show in another couple days, and we'd talked to reporters in Kenai and Homer already. Alaska is a small enough place that it's not too hard to be a minor celebrity. Complete strangers felt compelled to call CPS or proclaim we were terrible parents to our kids, while other complete strangers vigorously defended us. Why did we put ourselves out there? As backward as it seems, talking about yourself is a great way to start listening. If you're public—if you write about your life and let the newspaper do the same—people feel they know you. People want to say hi. They'll come up to you at a party, invite you into their home, start off asking questions, and end up answering them.

There was no other way I could ever have met so many people. No other way that I could take a question like "What is the future of Alaska?" and spin it into a web of fascinating conversations. I bet we'll see surf shops in the Aleutians, someone said. Alaska is parked at a global crossroads between Asian markets and Arctic shipping routes. Alaska has fresh water when everywhere else is running out. People will come to Alaska because it'll still have winter when other places don't. People will come to Alaska because it's one of the only wild places left. The state will get warmer and we'll suck up every last drop of oil. They'll come to Anchorage from drought-stricken California and they'll come from Alaska's dying rural villages, but of course they'll come.

It takes a true optimist to spin our wet and cold as resources. Anchorage people seemed more optimistic than any other Alaskans we'd talked to. The boomtown aura still hangs over the skyscrapers and the urban moose that cross the streets between them. How could it not, in a city that started with such a bang and is now 150 times bigger? Seattle, my own hometown, is just three times more populous than it was in 1915. From the streets of Anchorage, it seems inevitable that things will continue hurtling along the same trajectory, like the four lanes of traffic streaking past.

There is a concept, brought from Europe, of "forest kinder-gartens," where small children forgo school buildings to learn entirely in the great outdoors. People send me links to articles about this concept, drawing the obvious parallel to my own children. It is a similar set of people who quote the line "There's no bad weather, only bad clothing." Have they ever been in blowing sleet? Do they build those schools where it snows like this in May?

Snow stuck to the rotted leaves beside the sidewalk, leaving sugar-sprinkled patches between the gray and brown. Fat blobs of sleet pelted Katmai's bright orange hood and rolled down the side of the coat, slick and wet and glowing in strips where the headlights hit the reflective tape. If we'd been anywhere else but Anchorage, we wouldn't be walking. We'd have looked at the weather, shrugged, frowned, and set up camp early to wait out the miserable. Not possible on a parking strip. The next house was six miles away.

I draped a sleeping bag over my head and shoulders, giving Lituya an extra boost of warmth. I turned the heads of driver after driver, their vehicles crashing down into the sleety puddles and spraying us with their icy swash. The headlights were on against the thick sleet, and they didn't mean to splash, they just passed by so quickly, several every second, that the drivers didn't have time to think. My hands slowly chilled and I gripped the edges of the sleeping bag with stiff waterlogged claws, and the cars streamed by until the bubble of growth seemed infinite to me too, and I couldn't imagine where so many people needed to be so quickly.

But Anchorage was almost behind us. We were nearing Knik Arm. We were as prepared as we could be. I'd spent hours in a hotel room next to the midtown shopping malls going back and forth and back and forth between the room and the sprawling sports stores across the road, toting shopping bags of shoes and coats of different sizes. Katmai had shredded his raingear and outgrown his sleeping bag. Hig's sleeping pad was toast. Maybe water shoes would work better for the kids to hike in, since they walked in every available puddle and stream. And speaking of water, we might need to carry more fresh water to cross the Susitna Delta. We'd definitely need to carry a solar charger for the far side of the inlet, where only one town and scattered fishing cabins would interrupt the rest of our journey.

We piled it up on our last host's scale. The food. The water. The gear. Have to count Lituya as well, of course, since she's part of the load. If you add it all together, 140 pounds. Hig and I split that weight between us, but still. . . . I scribbled down the categories in red crayon on an envelope and went back to weigh it all again. That can't be right. It was our last chance to leave things behind before we left town, but I couldn't think of anything in the pile I was sure we could do without. Sometimes keeping hold of the two-year-old in parking lots seems like the hardest part of journeying with children. Sometimes it's the blowing sleet. Wipe that away and you're left with the sheer staggering incontrovertible weight of it all.

We staggered, and ached, but we could stand. And maybe the boomtown aura infected me too, because it seemed inevitable that we'd just continue hurtling along the same trajectory, the expedition distance melting away beneath our overburdened feet and scratched-up paddles. Knik Arm loomed ahead, guarding the entrance to Cook Inlet's west side with two miles of rushing tides and who-knows-what weather. I was excited to begin.

Tidal rapids slice through the mudflats near the Susitna Delta.

THE OCEAN'S FEATHERED EDGE

MAY 22–27: ANCHORAGE TO TYONEK

On Knik Arm, on the shore of Anchorage, low tide doesn't smell like the fizzing waves of drying seaweed and rotting snails. This far up Cook's "River," tides of silt bury anything that dares to live on the bottom. Here, low tide smells like mud and exhaust. Shipping containers and loading cranes rise behind the metal sea walls. Skyscrapers loom and bicycles whiz by on the Coastal Trail's ribbon of pavement. The trail is a bright-line boundary between urban and wild.

I don't usually enter into battles with inanimate geography, but Knik Arm and I had some unfinished business to resolve. On an expedition five years earlier, Knik Arm had fended Hig and me off with a crushing mass of ice floes, smashed and scrambled in the same tidal currents that had halted Captain Cook's ships. It was minus twenty degrees then. Today was just cold enough for a jacket and hat, and Knik Arm led with its fortification of mud. It stretched before us, a slick gray expanse rippled and cracked and pocked by bird tracks. There can be quicksand here too. Also gooey mud and gloppy mud, quivering mud and hardened mud, slippery mud and sinking mud. One step leaves a gorgeously clear sneaker print. And the next?

"Mommmm!" Katmai stood like a teetering crane in a puffy down coat—one foot in the mud, the other, held up with a bent knee, displaying a sock that once was blue. I plunged my hands into the muck, fished out the tiny "water shoe" we'd just bought him, and smeared it back onto his foot. A couple of minutes later, I did the same for Lituya.

Anchorage friends stood by on slightly more solid ground, while I bent over, puffing the last breaths of air into the packraft, distractedly pushing my hair out of my eyes. A bell rang. I waved back at the cyclist, my face a war-paint of mud and sunblock. Then we entered Knik Arm in a slippery rush, the weight of Lituya and the backpack almost sending my packraft to sea before I could jump in. I pulled my foot out of calf-deep mud to slide down several feet of mud bank and into a low-tide canyon. The current pulsed through a narrowing rush of muddy walls. Anchorage was behind us, invisible now. The packrafts fit, just barely, our paddles scraping the channel walls, sending mini-landslides of mud into the water.

I couldn't see Hig and Katmai ahead of us. Lituya and I bounced around each corner of the winding canyon, our boat following the rapids that poured down layer after layer of mud. I followed the tide that sliced these Vs through the mudflats until I caught up to Hig, bumping into the back of his raft. He was levering his paddle blades against the channel walls, trying to shove the raft forward. We came to a standstill, a packraft logjam. Water built up behind our boats, funneling over Hig's stern in a rush to join the ocean.

"Go, Mom! Go!" Lituya cheered, gesturing with a fistful of potato chips. Her nose and cheeks were already the color of Knik Arm. I scooched. I wiggled. I pushed off, carving slabs of buttery mud into the channel and sending gray splashes over us both. The water swelled behind us until it finally shot our packrafts into the sea like some sort of digestive blockage.

We floated side by side in the calm. Hig fished out the cell phone, dripping, from a raincoat pocket. We paddled two miles. The tide took us a few more, pulling us another mile out into the inlet before pushing us back up to Point MacKenzie, on the far side of Knik Arm. Point MacKenzie bulges south toward the cupped northern shore of downtown Anchorage, squeezing the sprawling inlet into a strait only a couple of miles wide. The bow of my packraft nudged the gravel shore, and I raised my arms in a mocking cheer. Triumph! "We have vanquished Knik Arm!"

Hig laughed. "Knik Arm has vanquished our cell phone. Probably." He tucked the black-screened rectangle back in a pocket. "Can't check yet. But nothing's dead until we try and dry it out by the fire. Many electronics have been saved that way."

I spun the boat back to face Anchorage, pausing the conversation while a jet shrieked its way aloft from the Anchorage airport. The kids had fallen asleep on our laps, and it seemed unwise to clamber out and wake them. Knik Arm rose slowly around us. I lay back into the smooth brown flood, watching the airplanes, paddling a stroke or two every few minutes to keep myself grounded on the shore. Knik Arm was the apogee of our journey, the point where we turned from civilization back to wilderness. Yet for all its mud and currents, Knik Arm was only two miles wide. The spot we'd actually been worried about—scheming about for months, poring over maps with no useful details and Google Earth photos painted in unknowable shades of greenish-grayish-brown—was just ahead. The Susitna Flats.

At the Susitna River, tides flow seven miles up from the mouth, which is seven miles wide, where fifty-one thousand cubic feet of water rush past each second. That makes it the fifteenth largest river in the country. It also made the Susitna a travel corridor. Each spring, probably about the time we bumped against this shore, the Dena'ina who lived at its mouth came down to this spot—Point MacKenzie—to trade hooligan fish with the Dena'ina of Knik Arm. All of them knew—easily—how to navigate the thirty miles of mudflats and swirling tidal currents of this region. We did not.

We clambered out to try it anyway. Point MacKenzie's gravel beach ended in a drift line of winter's casualties, just beginning to thaw. One of the porcupine carcasses had its quills plucked out. The moose was a crumple of leg bones, collared at the ankle with coarse hair, hooves still attached. Lituya stroked the dusty hair. Katmai crawled in and out of the burst-out windows of tilting duck-hunting shacks, their weathered wood crumbling into the drift line. Two live porcupines bristled at our presence and waddled up the wooded slope. The gravel beach ended in a shimmery warning, where the ocean feathered, wet and edgeless, into the grassy marshlands beyond. If we walked out there, where could we stop? We'd be as likely to camp in a puddle as anything else. If the tide didn't flood it all.

"Maybe we *should* take the four-wheeler trail." I probed the thigh-deep, six-foot-wide slough with a stick. A few minutes later, we were wading through ankle-deep water to the wooded back edge of the marsh, where the trail wove through ruts of ice water, black spruce forest, and tundra that would have been spongy if it weren't frozen.

Wrong choice. Ever spent long hours wading across the land with perpetually soggy feet? Days? Weeks? I can tell you, it's all in the temperature of the water. That's the difference between the sob-inducing intensity of a slush bath and the tromping joy of a woolly mammoth platypus. We backtracked, to a warmer sogginess. The water pooled on the mudflats was warm enough that I didn't even mind waiting, ankle-deep, while Katmai-the-woolly-mammoth-platypus stomped on the knobs of wobbly brown grass that poked above the water and Lituya slithered across the lichen on weathered logs and rotten boats.

Tall brown reeds marked water so deep that you'd best avoid it—even warm. The flat-bladed grass tussocks weren't too wobbly for walking. Short grass bristled beneath a few inches of warm water, firm and springy underfoot. Golden rye grass sprayed clouds of silt dust with every footstep. And when the grass feathered away into salty ocean, there was nothing left but the mud. I ran out of words that meant "gooey." It was more fun to compare this world to food. The frosting that lines the channel banks. The softened butter beneath my paddles. The layers of canned pumpkin or pureed squash, tomato sauce or heavy cream, stacked up into a sensory smorgasbord of dirtiness. The mudflats might even be lovable. But they did not, in fact, have a single dry spot to fit a tent on.

We camped on a duck shack porch. In every square inch of mud, there were bird tracks. In every moment of silence, there were bird songs. Cranes, gulls, snipes, shorebirds, ducks, and geese. They were here in the spring and they'd be here in the fall, with hunters following close behind. The state gives people permits to put up cabins out here where no one lives—perched on pilings above the tide—because the hunters can't find a dry campsite either. Across the water, Anchorage's downtown skyscrapers gleamed pink in the light of the sunset. Houses sprawled up the hillside above the city, sparkling streetlamp orange beneath alpenglow peaks. Over the wind farms of Fire Island, a full moon rose. And if you're seeing all of that in late May, it means you're staying up pretty darn late.

"We walked at least five miles, but I think we made about two miles of actual progress," I commented later that night, squinting at the map.

"About what I thought," Hig replied, dangling his bare feet over the edge of the porch, sweaty gray soup streaming between his fingers as he squeezed out the tattered remains of his socks.

"Why don't you just switch socks now?" I asked him. "I bet you could even burn those—they're wool."

"Because this environment is really hard on socks. If I can get across the Susitna Flats—"

"And the Trading Bay Flats, and the Tuxedni Bay Flats, and the Chinitna Bay Flats," I interrupted.

"We'll have it all figured out by then," he said. "We won't be wandering around like idiots, we'll be—"

"Muddy."

Hig laughed. "Mudflat experts."

In 1896—it was May then too—Mr. W. A. Dickey got off a steamship, picked his way around ice blocks on the beach, clambered into an open dory with a few partners, and pushed off with the tide. Channels braided, crisscrossed, unmappable. It took them two days to find the mouth of the Susitna. The tide swept them upriver, until finally they reached the current that tumbled out of the glaciers, too strong for their boats. So they stopped and whipsawed lumber to make two river boats, caulked them over with spruce gum and grease, and pushed on upstream, wading through the cold, tugging a thousand pounds of supplies in each boat, hoping to make a couple of miles each day. We had digital maps, instant communication, and gear so light the miners wouldn't recognize it, but we went about as far, in a day, as they had. The miners were only here to get rich. Their goal was material wealth, their commodity was largely useless to the world, and they were one of the forces that decimated the people who lived here first. The world would probably be better off if every speck of their gold was still buried beneath a ton of gravel. Still, it was hard not to admire their ingenuity.

The next morning, I repacked the diapers and walked back inside the duck shack, Lituya on my hip. Katmai slept while we packed around him. He could sleep in the packraft, but who wakes such a sweetly sleeping child? That blond head, that muddy face, those unknowable dreams. Water poured down the sloughs, racing away from us as we struggled to catch up, struggled to get ready in time for the tide. It was 9:42 a.m. At 7:42 a.m. the tide had stood at 32.4 feet, leaving just a few patches of grass above the water. At 3:03 p.m. the tide would stand at minus 4.2 feet. That difference adds up to more than 36 feet of water—enough to flood the entire tip of Florida. Here it just left us with a tide flat that seemed Florida-sized, with water in a rushing hurry to cross it, four times a day.

The loose and lagging rhythm of family camping was a grating contrast to the specificity of the tide tables. Tides feel so big and messy—as overwhelming as the weather. It has always astonished me that we can predict them so exactly. That I can look up just where the water will stand in a certain spot at a certain time, months or even years into the future. Any periodic motion can be calculated as the sum of a number of simpler curves. In 1867 the English mathematician Sir William Thompson applied this to the tides. Only mathematicians noticed. By hand, the math was too monstrous to be of any use. In 1881, William Ferrel designed a tide prediction machine for the US Coast and Geodetic Survey. At eleven feet long and over twenty-five hundred pounds, it was a mechanical marvel of gears and dials, capable of summing thirty-seven different components of the tide—adjustable for each tide location—to spit out the same sort of numbers now printed in a free book that fits in my pocket. The Dena'ina didn't have tide books, of course. Nor did Captain Cook, the steamship drivers, the gold rush prospectors, the early fishermen, or the homesteaders. In 1922, Anchorage had a part-time tidal observation station. Everyone else had to know tides for themselves.

They had to take the tides by feel. The incremental shifting—about forty-five minutes later each day. The increasing drama of stronger currents, clam beds laid bare and flooding marshes as the full and new moons drew near. Tides move across the earth as a wave, bulging, reflecting, interfering with each other as they bounce off the intricate outlines of the land and resonate in enclosed pockets like Cook Inlet. Tides can sweep you, shove you, ground you. Captain Cook filled his logs with notes on the tide, on the time the ebb began each day, the force of the current, the fathoms of water, or lack of water, beneath his ship. His ships flowed with the current because they couldn't fight the tide any more than our packrafts could. The highest average tidal range in the world is thirty-eight feet, in Canada's Bay of Fundy. Cook Inlet's average range is thirty feet.

"It will appear," Cook wrote, "from what has been said occasionally of the tide, that it is considerable in this river and contributes very much to facilitate the navigation of it. It is high-water in the stream, on the days of the new and full moon, between two and three o'clock; and the tide rises, upon a perpendicular, between three and four fathoms. The reason of the tide's being greater here, than at other parts of this coast, is easily accounted for. The mouth of the river being situated in a corner of the coast, the flood that comes from the ocean is forced into it by both shores, and by that means swells the tide to a great height."

It was a full moon. More than two hundred years later, our low tide was at the same time Cook's high had been, and four fathoms—twenty-four feet—was an understatement. I closed my tide book, shouldered my backpack, and grabbed Katmai's hand. It was after 11 a.m. by the time we felt our way down to the slough, slipping and sliding down the glistening mud banks, my paddle as a brake. We flopped into the packrafts and followed the slough. Ducks erupted from the water, scared up at every curve. The mud canyon became a creek, then a river whose banks we could now see over, then, in a foaming rush, it became the ocean.

It was 12:30 by now. We crossed a choppy eddy line where brown foam churned and boiled, gathering up sticks and logs of driftwood. We were flying. Rushing. Racing. Sprinting. Perhaps it takes a couple months of walking at the speed of a four-year-old to appreciate it, but five miles an hour is really *fast*. The energy is overwhelming.

Calculations show that 90 percent of the tidal energy potential in the United States is in Alaska—and much of that is in Cook Inlet, where shallow constricted channels and high tidal ranges combine into the rush we were following. Alaskans might power half our "Railbelt" (the road-connected cities from Homer to

Fairbanks) with the tide. But silt scours anything you put in this brown water, as it scours our skin and our tent zippers. Ice floes shatter and crash for months out of the year. Neutrally buoyant ice chunks, as big as boxcars, have been described as "bowling balls coming down the inlet." Just imagine them crashing into a turbine. Alaska is energetic—violently energetic.

As early as the 1950s, other engineers looked to the energy of the Susitna River itself. Its hydroelectric potential was studied and dropped, and studied and dropped again, and now resurrected in a six-billion-dollar plan to build a six-hundred-megawatt power plant and a thirty-square-mile dam, stopping the giant Susitna where rapids boil through the Wantana Canyon, 184 miles upstream. If built, the dam might be a way to cut some of the web of ties that binds Alaska to its fossil fuels. Or it might be hubris. A pork-barrel boondoggle and the sure death of salmon. Depending on which Alaskan you talk to.

Water hit the base of Katmai's sand castle. It undermined the crumbling foundation, curled around the walls, and poured into the space behind them. He clutched his paddle-shovel, watching the flood. The dropping tide had pulled us down the slough, from the duck shack to the ocean, to the sandbar. We'd paused for lunch, and now the tide was coming back. The island was gone. It was a stream of hissing bubbles ascending to the surface through the rising tide. Eruptions of water shot several inches into the air. A dozen belugas joined us at the edge of the current, whooshing and splashing as they fed in the eddy line. Their spouts arced above the rising tide. Watching them, I could imagine the salmon flooding with the tide, swimming right into those great white mouths.

"Susitna" comes from the Dena'ina word *Suyitnu*, meaning "Sand River." I wonder if they named it for someplace far upstream of the mudflats, where rippled sandbars broke the river into braids. Or from when they paddled out here, where sandy islands appeared and disappeared with the tide, and river and ocean blended into one. Mirages stretched the distant mountains into a city of skyscrapers, hovering above a cushion of mirror-like water. Trees floated on nothing, some uncountable number of miles away.

We were in the middle of the ocean. That was my most precise estimate of our location. The cell phone drowned by Knik Arm had been partially resurrected by a campfire, and when I found enough power and signal to turn it on, shaded the wonky rippled screen with a hand, and turned on the online tracking app, I could sometimes actually locate us in space. Otherwise? We were mere flotsam in the currents.

I'd told Hig the other night, "If we can cross the Susitna, we can do anything." But the Susitna wasn't something we could cross. Or fight. Or even drink. It was like a breathing giant, blowing us out in the morning, then snorting us back in at the end of the day. Exhaled with the driftwood, our packrafts streaking past mountains so fast it felt like we were one of those jets painting contrails in the sky. Then inhaled. Sucked in toward the shore, sucked back up into the Susitna, the tide rushing upstream as we tried to pick a channel that might help us get the right direction. We navigated by specks on the horizon. Nothing could tell us how far we were from shore, when the shore itself could grow or shrink by miles in a few brief hours. We just hoped to make it from the giant's left nostril to the right.

The Susitna was inhaling now. The air was as calm as the water was energetic. A brilliant May sun bounced off the waves, vibrating with heat that made us strip down to long underwear, wishing we had the sort of T-shirts we never brought on any Alaskan journey, no matter the season. I smeared more sunblock into the silt on Lituya's face. "No food for half an hour!" she sang cheerily, tossing a half-eaten granola bar over the edge of the raft, anticipating her punishment.

"Lituya, we only have a certain amount of food here. Will you be happy if it runs out?" She smirked at me, stuck her tongue out, and took a huge slurping lick of the backpack on our bow. "I want to go to shore!"

Previous page: Forced onto the mud by the currents of Chickaloon Bay, we rest our gear on the only dry surface available. *Above:* While we set up to packraft on Kachemak Bay, Lituya plays with a paddle. *Facing page, top*: Slush slicks the tide flats on the south side of Kachemak Bay, where we were caught in an April blizzard. *Facing page, bottom*: Coyote or fox tracks in the buttery mud of Turnagain Arm.

Facing page, top: We take a paddling break on a white beach made of barnacle shells, in the fjords of Kachemak Bay. *Facing page, bottom*: The full moon hangs over the Fire Island wind generators and the Chugach Range across Knik Arm. *Above*: The kids examine moose droppings on a snowy trail.

Facing page, top: The sun sets on a calm day, turning the water orange. *Facing page, bottom:* Niki's tent and our tent perch on a windy knob near Iliamna Bay. *Above:* A setnet fisherman fills a bowl with fresh salmon fillets—some for dinner, some to preserve.

Facing page, top: Near Point Possession, a small creek rushes over the tide flats, passing scattered glacial erratics. *Facing page, bottom*: Still snow-covered in late April, Mount Iliamna towers over Cook Inlet, and an oil rig probes beneath its waters. *Above*: Along Turnagain Arm, Lituya revels in the possibilities of mud.

Above: Mount Augustine puffs a cloud of steam, across the Douglas River tide flats and Kamishak Bay. *Facing page, top*: A brittle star snakes over seaweed during an extreme low tide at Scott Island, on the west side of Cook Inlet. *Facing page, bottom*: Katmai sleeps on Hig's lap, while I paddle in front of the rafts lashed together from below with a driftwood pole.

Facing page, top: Usually an alpine species, small colonies of marmots inhabit parts of Cook Inlet's rocky shores. *Facing page, bottom:* Spring bursts into bloom with Kamchatka rhododendrons, on the tundra cliffs above Kamishak Bay. *Above*: I paddle down a tidal channel of the Susitna River, with an oil platform visible in the fog beyond.

Above: A Monterey dorid (a shelless creature related to snails) glides through a tide pool on the Nanwalek reef. *Facing page, top*: A sign on the Nanwalek grocery store. *Facing page, bottom*: A field of dandelions blooms beneath setnets hung for repair on Chisik Island. *Last page*: One of our packrafts glides across the buttery mud of the Trading Bay flats.

Wet streaks of toddler spit formed lines and dots on the dusty gray backpack. "I see you're doing modern art now. I'll call this *Saliva on Silt #1*." *Saliva on Silt #2–10* kept us occupied for a good half an hour, as I found butterflies and mountains in her Rorschach blots of slobber. Katmai joined in from his perch in Hig's boat, both kids collapsing in gritty giggles.

We were still in the middle of the ocean, paddling toward shore as the tide rushed up over it. It was impossible to tell, in the moment, if we were getting closer or farther away. We paused on a sandbar. Just enough time to stretch our legs and pee before the ground turned soupy and the water rose over the toes of my shoes.

"Look Lituya! A little seal, swimming right toward us!" The water rose over our sandbar island, over the seal's island beside us. It came in an awkward hurry with a cry of "*raaarh, raaaaaah!*" nosing up first to Hig's packraft, then mine, as if our rafts were its long-lost mother.

"What is it *doing?!*" Lituya screeched.

"Trying to climb in . . . ," I guessed. "Don't touch it!" Baby seals are ridiculously cute. It nosed up to the sloping stern of my boat, flailing with its little flippers, nudging the tube with its snub nose. The water rose around us all. Hig and I paddled to another, slightly higher sandbar. So did the seal. It rolled in the sand, until its face, whiskers, and skinny body were decorated with clumps of grit. It had a quarter-sized lesion on its back. It shivered.

The water rose again. It swam to where adult seals bobbed in the current nearby, then back to our rafts, ping-ponging back and forth between my red raft and Hig's yellow one, crying so pitifully it almost set me crying myself. It hadn't mistaken us for its mother. It had mistaken us for land, desperately seeking a haulout on the slippery tubes of the rafts. The sun was warm. The water was cold. One by one, the sandbars were disappearing beneath the rush of the flood tide. Everything solid would soon be miles away.

I felt an almost irresistible temptation to reach out and help the little guy into the raft. What if I had some kind of a net, and . . . No. We were lucky that polyurethane is in fact too slippery—too slippery for me to find out what damage a baby seal the size of my toddler, with much sharper teeth, could do if it found itself on my lap. It followed us for a good ten minutes, porpoising up and down as it swam, trying to keep track of us in the silty water. Crying. Its speed matched ours. I couldn't help but feel relieved when it finally swam away for another sandbar, disappearing from view as our packrafts swept beyond it. Even there, it had only one more minute of dry land.

Then . . . Whose version of the story do you want to believe? I saw something tired and hopeless. I saw the doomed shortsightedness of that pup chasing after each disappearing sandbar, missing the inevitable—squandering the energy it could have used to swim to the real shore. Sometimes I feel that most humans act like that seal pup, swimming toward every new sandbar with a shortsighted hope that the world isn't changing after all, weaving back and forth for an extra five minutes above the water. Trying to ignore the tide.

But perhaps I'd been talking about the future with too many grown-ups. Katmai assured me: "There's this seal called the Perdonner Seal, and it finds baby seals that have been lost from their mothers, and it protects them and brings them to the Showing Seal." The baby would be cared for and taught. It would grow fat and practice fishing, until it swam back out of its mythical haven, strong and invincible.

Perhaps the reality is somewhere in between. Harbor seal pups are born every spring, and left every spring, by their foraging mothers. Perhaps they all cry with the tide. Perhaps they all cry as the world changes around them, like the kids whining each morning when they're told to put their shoes on. Perhaps they'll all find the shore in the end.

After a long cramped day in the boats, a thorough exploration of *Saliva on Silt* and every nursery rhyme I could remember, we were ready for shore ourselves. While following the tide to sea is a rushing experience of thrilling power, following it back to land is an experience of waiting around with ducks. The water covers the sandbars. Then the water pushes you beyond the sand, back into the realm of buttery mudflats and splintering channels. You pick a fork, guessing your way through a maze that soon ends in a rivulet of ankle-deep water and a rush of startled flapping.

We sat back down in our trickle, watching the bubbles jiggle back and forth on the water's surface until, finally, the water caught up and began to flow past us. Both kids had fallen asleep. Sandpipers prodded the banks beside us with their long beaks, walking faster than we could paddle. A flock of cranes winged past, adding their distinctive stuttering cry to the gulls and ducks we'd almost stopped listening to.

It felt like summer, but it sounded like spring. Far to the north, the Inupiat women used to sing songs to the first bird of each species returning in the spring. There's no more powerful magic, nothing quite so overwhelming as coming through all of that harsh cold and finding yourself surrounded, twenty-four hours a day, by the music of a thousand birds. We'd be making friends with mud for weeks or months to come.

But we were across the Susitna.

After a day of empty nets, the Standifer family prepares a single salmon, gifted by their neighbors.

THE BEACH
PEOPLE

MAY 28–29: TYONEK

A veiled brown curtain ran through the agate's smoky yellow. I rubbed my fingers across its knobbly surface before dropping it in my pocket, clattering against a half-dozen other agate pebbles I'd already collected. I was tempted to put them all in my pocket—not just the agates but all the gray and black and white stones too, every miraculous pebble that surrounded us.

We were beyond the Susitna Flats, walking a meandering path between wave-carried swashes of gravel and sand. Beside the scattered boulders, the beach rose sharply to a steep sandy bluff. Cottonwood trees lined up along the edge, brightened now by a fringe of yellowish green, and wafting their sticky-sweet scent into the air. Eagles perched in matted nests. Each time my foot thumped against the solidity of sand and rock, it felt like a miracle. We were walking on the *beach*.

The Dena'ina people who lived here called themselves Tubughna—the Beach People. It seems an apt description for a region where beaches are in such short supply. To the north and east, the coastline stretches across the vast mudflats of the Susitna Delta, the whorls and eddies of Knik and Turnagain arms. To the southwest are more mudflats, interspersed with a few peninsulas of sand, until the land turns to the steep cliffs of the Iniskin Peninsula and the harsh weather of Kamishak Bay.

In this spot there was dry sand. There was gravel. There were gently sloping uplands laced with clear rivers and creeks. Those don't seem like much of a resource, until you've been missing them a while. Until you've waded through the mud and paddled past the cliffs, and realize just how perfect this place is. From here, the Tubughna could access both the ocean and the land. They turned whole driftwood trees upside down in the flats, cabling them to the sand. As the tide rushed in, beluga whales followed the salmon up the rivers, and hunters harpooned them from platforms created by the upturned roots. This style of hunting was found nowhere else on earth. They perched on other buried trees to dipnet salmon straight from the ocean. They could travel down the coast to dig razor clams or up onto the land to hunt for their meals.

Eventually, to hunt for other things, the Tubughna could paddle out to the large hulking vessels of the folks they called the "Underwater People." They gave that name to the people on Captain Cook's ship, for the way the approaching sails appeared, on the horizon, to rise up from the sea. A flotilla of boats, the larger ones containing entire families, met Cook's ship when he anchored off their beaches in 1778, exchanging furs and fish for blue glass beads and the pieces of iron they asked for by Russian name.

Cook didn't linger here, bent on his task to seek the Northwest Passage. But Captains Nathaniel Portlock and George Dixon had both been members of Cook's first voyage into this "river." By the time their pair of sailing ships anchored just off this coast in 1786, the grandiose dreams of a Northwest Passage had been replaced by simple mercenary goals. Perhaps they imagined silky sea otter furs draped over their arms, or the clinking piles of gold each pelt could bring, or the fame and status they would bring back with their riches.

The Tubughna approached these new ships too, paddling alongside them waving green branches and breaking into song. But it only took a few days of trade to "drain the land of furs," resulting in Portlock impatiently waiting through a series of fresh gales that left him afraid to weigh anchor. Despite the weather, canoes still paddled past, landing deftly in conditions that kept the big ship at anchor. Portlock scoffed at the handful of salmon that was all they had to offer.

Perhaps the Russians had gotten all the furs already. The Tubughna who stepped aboard the English ships tried to trade unwanted Russian clothing to these new outsiders. An elderly chief's pantomimed story left Dixon certain that the Tubughna had recently bested the Russians in battle. He was equally certain that the quarrel must have started with some Native thievery. Their final visitor came to beg the Englishmen's assistance against the Russians—or Portlock thought he did. The captain refused this "importune" request: "to console him in some measure for this disappointment I gave him a light horseman's cap of which he was very proud and his countrymen beheld him with such a mixture of admiration and envy that I greatly question whether he will be able to keep it long in his possession. I also distributed a few trifles amongst the other Indians and they returned on shore perfectly satisfied."

Casting himself as the Tubughna's potential savior, Portlock may have been listening as much to his own prejudices— against Russians and Indians—as to the Dena'ina words he couldn't understand.

While English explorers swept through the inlet, hardly stepping off their boats, the Russian promyshlenniki spent years on each fur-hunting expedition. They solidified their foothold on the shores. In 1794, eight years after Portlock and Dixon's expedition, Captain Vancouver's men ducked into the single long building that housed nineteen Russians at Tyonek and staggered at the stench. They clutched their stomachs, pushed away dried fish and cranberries offered to them, and almost ran for the fresh air of their own tents. How could the Russians live there without cultivating gardens or improving their situation? For four years?

To Vancouver's eyes, the Russians were nearly as uncivilized as the Indians. Perhaps they deserved each other. "The Russians seemed to live upon the most intimate terms of friendship with the Indians of all descriptions," he wrote, "who appeared to be perfectly satisfied in being subjected to the Russian authority." The Dena'ina disagreed with this assessment, and a few years later, Chief Quq'ey led the Tubughna to destroy the fort, as other Dena'ina destroyed the larger establishment near the Kenai River. The upper inlet was, in the words of Alexander Baranov, the head of the Russian American Company, an "administrative nuisance."

There never were sea otters here. The few skins Portlock and Dixon came away with in 1786 must have been acquired through travel or trade. Sea otters don't live in the muddy waters of the upper inlet. They can't handle the winter's ice. But even without sea otters, the ships still came. By the time Vancouver arrived, the Dena'ina he encountered were no strangers to Europeans. They knew how to make a good impression. It was a hungry time of spring, and even as the Natives knew how to paddle through the grinding ice floes that terrified the captain, they also knew how to catch a ride up the inlet on Vancouver's ship. They knew how to come away with some of the Europeans' food despite having nothing much to trade for it. The Dena'ina left Vancouver convinced they were "a people unactuated by ambition, jealousy, or avarice."

They would need all the savvy they could get. The destroyed Russian outpost was soon replaced. And for the next hundred or so years, sailboats called at the trading post of Tyonek. When the steamships came, they didn't brave the Turnagain Arm tidal bores or the Knik Arm shallows. They skipped the swirling currents and mud of the Susitna Delta. They disgorged their prospectors, their supplies, and their diseases on the Tubughna's beach.

"Look Katmai, I see another Slug-a-saurus up ahead!" He dropped my hand, setting off in a run that lapped against the edges of the tide, in and out of tiny waves, small splashes interspersed with the wet slap of shoes on gravel. "I'm going to jump off it!" He scrambled to the top of the boulder—the Slug-a-saurus—and jumped. Both arms stretched to catch the hand Hig extended to him. I looked for the next rock the glaciers had left behind. The shadow of the bluffs fell on Katmai's pale skin. We'd let him go shirtless, on an evening that was hot but no longer skin-scorching. Lituya slumped against my shoulder, asleep. Her hot sticky heat melted into my back. Hig carried Katmai's tiny purple backpack hooked onto his own monstrous load. The Slug-a-sauruses, the jumping . . . All we wanted was a few more miles out of those small legs.

It was late enough to camp, but we couldn't yet. "Step *over* the rope," I hissed at Katmai, waving hello to a couple at the top of the beach relaxing beside their four-wheeler. Instead, he reached down to grab the line. "What is—"

"A fishing net. Come on." I grabbed Katmai's hand and turned back toward the couple. "We're going to Frank Standifer's fish camp," I said, quickly slipping past them. It was as much a defense as it was a piece of small talk.

"Relax," Hig said as soon as they were out of earshot. "Just be friendly. We're invited." We were approaching the current home of the Tubughna—the village of Tyonek, home to around 150 people. It's only forty miles from Anchorage, but no road can reach it. It's the only town on the western side of Cook Inlet. Southwest of Tyonek, 650 miles of bear-strewn coast separates it from the next town—Chignik. It's the longest stretch of unpeopled coastline in the entire state of Alaska, which makes it, easily, the longest stretch of unpeopled coastline in the country.

Like most villages its size, Tyonek has a post office, a gas station, and a school. It has a gravel airstrip, where pilots land to unload the cases of soda and diapers that fill the shelves of the village store. These items are, of course, expensive. And you are not allowed to show up and buy them. Tyonek is a closed village. You can't just walk in. Or fly in. Or snow machine or four-wheel in. Tyonek will only let you in if you have a local sponsor. We'd been invited by Chief Frank Standifer, courtesy of work Hig had done with Frank's daughter. But today, Frank was at his fish camp, three miles down the beach from the village proper. That's where we needed to get.

We paused where a road led up to the village. Lituya pushed a small blocky stone along the gravel, softly narrating the journey of her rock car along the winding furrow it dug into the beach. Just above us, the overlapping ruts of four-wheelers and dirt bikes made this coast a real enough thoroughfare. I leaned back against the warm rocks, crunching down on a granola bar. The too-sweet oats shattered between my teeth.

"Eat up," Hig said. "My pack is heavy." It was. It left a dent in the beach—a small crater—each time he set it down. It was our one pack for four people, straining every stitch line with the granola bars, spaghetti, and nuts we'd stuffed in the day before. The resupply box had been sent to friends who lived at a homestead just a few miles up the inlet from Tyonek, so we'd eaten only a day's worth of the nearly two weeks of food it contained. The resupply would have to last us to the end of the next mudflat. We knew how mud and tides could go. It was best to be prepared.

Hig leaned back against the pack and murmured about his aching shoulders. I carried Lituya, so he had to bear the brunt of the load. With the new load-lifter straps he'd added to his pack in Anchorage, he was a little better off, but only a little. He is the most optimistic, least-complaining person I know. Even now, he complained only a little, channeling most of the discomfort into well-articulated arguments in favor of packrafting, any day it was possible, so he didn't have to shoulder that load. He'd never say no to an expedition, no matter how difficult, if at least some of the difficulty was exciting and new.

The Susitna Flats were exciting and new, and they'd made up for some of the trudging boredom of the parallel highway portion. The wilder country was up ahead, and even as the longer stretches between resupply points made the pack even heavier, the challenge and novelty easily won him over. Or was it the summer? It was hard for any of us not to feel content. The lazy heat sunk into our bones, until even the kids play was only a murmur and a soft scraping of pebbles. It would have been easier if Frank had been at the village today. We thought we'd be done walking already, but our host was still miles ahead of us. Just a few more minutes of rest. The tide was wrong for paddling. I passed another granola bar to the kids.

People wandered down the short road from the village. Even if they didn't suspect us of showing up uninvited, the muddy family of white people attracted conversation. One man wondered how old the kids were. A woman stopped by to ask where we'd come from. She turned to look back toward the head of Cook Inlet, contemplating our route. "You know," she offered, "the elders used to get to Ship Creek in a day, when a potlatch was called there." Anchorage now squats right on top of Ship Creek, six days back by our mudflat meanderings. But I'd felt those tides. I imagined a paddler with the confidence to venture farther from those shores—a paddler who knew the tides in his bones. I had no trouble at all believing her. Even if all the food I'd stuffed in that resupply box betrayed a rather lesser confidence in our own speed of travel.

I shuffled a few feet forward, paused, and looked back at where Katmai was on his knees in the ocean, giggling at the results of a "fall" that looked suspiciously like a game. "Come on, Katmai— just two more miles to go!" We were almost at Frank's fishing camp—the last landmark loomed overhead. It was a wide cement causeway, thrust over a thousand feet out into the inlet, ending in a giant T. Water curled around a line of metal support pillars, streaming back toward Anchorage with the tide. The oil and gas dock wedged itself between fishing sites.

We passed several more fishing sites. They didn't look like much. A rope or a few of them, anchored to a rock or a tree at the top of the beach, stretched taut a foot or two above the gravel, to the water's edge and then out beyond it, to a buoy bobbing just offshore. A necklace of floats held a line at the top of the water, while a necklace of weights, invisible, held another line at the bottom. A net hung between them, a lattice of diamonds sized to catch a salmon's head. This was the long-anticipated opening of the king salmon subsistence season—the first chance to catch the early salmon returning to Cook Inlet this year. It seemed like all of Tyonek was out on the beaches, using one of the three days per week that the State Fish and Game agency had granted them.

Frank and Sue Standifer were chewing homemade snuff in front of a small plywood shack, in a neighborhood of shacks at the end of Tyonek's beaches. Frank's dark hair bristled with silver. Sue's was jet black with a stripe of white at the roots. Both wore loose long-sleeved shirts against the bugs that summer had brought, ready for the salmon they hoped summer would bring. It was May, but everyone called it summer, because the weather trumps the calendar any day. Their snuff was made of birch bark fungus burnt to ashes, mixed with tobacco into a concoction the Anchorage police did not always believe was benign. They laughed as they traded stories of being stopped—suspected of carrying something less local and less legal.

It seemed like most of Frank and Sue's possessions were sitting in front of the plywood shack. There was a cast iron pan as wide as a bike wheel, buckets in every color, lawn chairs and knives and the disassembled pieces of machines. The colorful eruption of grass and plastic reminded me of my driveway in August, of a space weighed down by the accumulation of a life lived outside.

Frank's grandson, Rocky, a stocky seven-year-old, was playing with his friend in a sandbox that might have contained a hundred plastic trucks and digging machines, their oranges and yellows ranging from eye-popping new to cracked and sun-faded. "Rocky can drive a real backhoe too," Frank pointed out proudly. Drivers' licenses are not required to drive on Tyonek's private roads, in the forty thousand acres of land the Native Corporation owns surrounding the village.

The history of land settlements in Alaska is different than in the Lower 48. Homesteaders marked their corners. The government built military bases and roads. The newcomers took plenty of land from the Natives, but no one signed any treaties for it. In 1959, Alaska became a state. The law allowed the new state government to choose lands for itself—those deemed "vacant"—from what the federal government had bought from Russia and believed it owned. Native territory was supposed to be left out of the deal, but the Natives weren't the ones deciding what constituted "vacant." Oil was found up in Prudhoe Bay in 1968, and the conflict boiled up into a fresh urgency. No pipeline could be built without first resolving land claims.

By then it had gotten a little harder for people to just snatch the land they wanted. By the 1960s the philosophy of the country had shifted a little. The corporate world was the paradigm of the day. The Alaska Federation of Natives believed their members would need to become capitalists to survive the new future. Instead of reservations, the Native Alaskans ended up with corporations. The Alaska Native Claims Settlement Act was passed in 1971, dividing the state into corporations that controlled forty-four million acres—a ninth of the land—and $963 million. Twelve large regional corporations owned land and minerals, and hundreds of small village corporations just owned land—like the land around Tyonek.

It only took two minutes before our children were presented with toys and candy. Maybe five minutes before they were playing in the sandbox, shyly at first, then slowly responding to the older kids' effort to include them. I've stumbled into dozens of Native Alaskan villages over the years—spending one day here, a few there, before stuffing some food in my pack and heading back out into the wilderness. Which leaves me qualified to generalize about pretty much nothing. Except for this: kids are welcome. Really welcome.

Katmai's pack barely fit his present—a plastic helicopter that had once been remote-controlled, its delicate black rotors spinning with the touch of his finger. Hig got a ride into town to wash soiled diaper covers and cheese-covered shirts. No one was in a hurry. Nothing in camp was neat or perfect or quiet or on time, and the kids didn't have to be either. It was heaven. The next morning, we ate pancakes from Sue's giant cast iron pan. Frank's son drove all the way to town just to fill up our water bottles and brought back a box bulging with cherries, strawberries, and oranges for the kids—far more than two preschoolers could possibly eat. The cherry juice was sticky and sweet, and even without knowing the expense of getting cherries way out here, it would have tasted like gold.

Frank and Sue's fish camp had everything they might want— except fish. "You used to be able to put a net in the water and get thirty or forty fish," Frank recalled.

"I know," one of his neighbors chimed in. "It's my anniversary tomorrow, and every anniversary, I was dealing with fish. Now I've got nothing."

They ran through the tally of everyone's luck. One family ended up with five fish. Another with three. Another with one. Everyone else, like Frank and Sue, came home that day with big fat zeros. The family who'd ended up with three fish stopped by to give them one. Rocky and Sue stood by with glum expressions, in the dim midnight light, watching Frank fillet that single fish. Everybody in Cook Inlet had been talking about how the king salmon were in trouble. The previous summer, Cook Inlet king runs, along with those in the Yukon and Kuskokwim rivers, had prompted an official disaster declaration. The commercial fishermen had talked about it defensively—assuring us it wasn't their fault. Other people had said it with concern or puzzlement. Here, they sounded like they'd never expected anything different.

Frank and Sue's fish camp had everything—except a future. Usually, the first answer to our question "What will the future here be?" was a pause, a dissembling. A shrugging I-don't-know that gave the person a chance to think it through. Frank had no such hesitation: "It sucks." Sue and all the neighbors gathered around the fire murmured a hearty agreement.

"They talk about economic development. But we've been there and done that, and you see what happens . . . Our culture was the first to be impacted here. Our fish are depleted. We didn't even catch one king today. Fish and Game keeps cutting down the openings. They're only six hours and they always make them on outgoing tides—so the fish aren't even coming up along the shore. The wood chip mill destroyed the silver run in the creek by putting gravel and birch bark over the wetlands, and brought in lots of new bugs on that ship. There's only going to be more development. I don't think it will turn around."

There were the Russians and the explorers. There were the prospectors and the loggers. And when the outsiders got done with those resources, they only found more. Tyonek is the only town in 650 miles of coast. But you don't make a closed-door policy if no one is trying to get in. A network of roads and pipelines sprawls out around Tyonek. The village is connected to the natural gas power plant at Beluga, which powers most of Anchorage. It's connected to a controversial coal mine proposal. It's connected to gas wells and oil wells and an oil workers' camp just a couple of miles from where we were sitting.

Tyonek wasn't always the only town on the inlet's western shore. There were villages up along the Susitna River and down the coast to Kustatan. All of them struggled. After the 1918 flu pandemic, there were only six or seven Tyonek people left. So they traveled up and down to the other dwindling villages and recruited more. The name Tubughnen—Beach Land—is so basic that scholars think it must have been the first beach on Cook Inlet that the Dena'ina ever reached. They're still here. Tyonek intends to survive.

Mist hovers over the tide flats of Trading Bay, where slippery mud lets Hig pull our gear in the packraft, hand in hand with Katmai.

THE OIL MEN

MAY 30–JUNE 6: TYONEK TO DRIFT RIVER

"Wait, where are you going again?"

"Cape Douglas," I explained, running my finger across the map on the cabin wall, bending over, then squatting down, until I went right off the edge of the laminated paper, tracing an imaginary line down to the floor and beyond.

"Whoa. That's impressive," said Alex, a setnet fisherman and lifelong Alaskan I'd met a few minutes ago as I walked past his cabin. "I mean, that's really far."

"Not so far. We started back at Dogfish Bay, back in March." For that, I had to gesture toward an entirely different part of the cabin. Part of me felt flattered by his comments. But really, I felt like we were over that hump. We had come much too far already for someone to be marveling at how far we still had to go. I took Alex's gift of string, salmon, and a filled-up water bottle and walked back to our tent to tuck them away, wriggling through the foot-wide gap between the tent edge and the sand. Zippers and sand don't mix. Or rather, they mix so thoroughly that it's nearly impossible to unmix them and ever slide the zipper again. The kids had always preferred to roll under the edge of the tent to get in. Now we followed them.

Alex and Abby's cabin marked the last patch of beach before the Trading Bay mudflats. Four-wheeler trails and roads followed the trees here, curving far inland toward gas wells and hunting spots. It was high tide, and everything reflected the sky, the ocean indistinguishable from the water-slicked mud. Alex was impressed by our plans. The Nigerian oil camp worker whom I'd spoken to a half hour earlier, two weeks into his first Cook Inlet job, had no idea what we were even talking about, as Hig rattled off place-names the worker had never heard. Neither had any relevant advice. Skiffs carry the fishermen. Planes and helicopters carry the oil workers. Somewhere beneath us, barrels of crude oil crossed the Trading Bay mudflats in the guts of a thick metal pipe. We had rafts and sneakers.

The next morning, the tide was low, and the wind was up. Thousands of miniature waves rippled over the shoals, frothing and crashing in endless lines of white. Not that six inches of water can get anyone in trouble. We tried to raft, like we usually tried to raft, for speed, for convenience, for Hig's aching shoulders. But as far as we could squint, beyond the two and a half miles of shallows, there were only more whitecaps beyond. We turned around, surfing the shoal waves onto a smear of mud, where Bonaparte gulls dove for fish in two inches of water. I slowly disentangled my legs from Lituya's sleeping body, and climbed out. The brown water lapped at my toes. What next? Prop the sleeping child on my pack in the water and roll up the packraft? Wait for high tide and paddle to shore?

Hig grabbed the long string connecting his paddle to his raft and tugged it sideways. I reached down to give my own raft an experimental tug. It moved! The kid, the pile of water bottles, and the huge bag of food pushed the floor of the raft down to the muddy bottom. And yet, it moved. Gliding. Sliding. Plowing along as if the mud was put there just to lubricate our way. We could walk *without* carrying packs or kids. We followed the edge of the dropping tide, leaving a pair of wide furrows beside the feathery impressions of flounder fins, the raised squiggles of worm casts, and the footprints of pigeon-toed ducks.

"Our goal is to get more muddy!" It was Katmai who yelled it but Lituya who took the challenge to heart. She thrust her arms in up to her elbows then pulled them out, glistening with a fresh coat of dripping gray. "Look at my new gloves!" she called.

Fog streamed over the flats the ocean had left behind, evaporating the last of the wetness, blowing a moist salt wind across our mud-caked legs. Drop something and the mud disguises it. Leave something and the tide covers it. There aren't even enough landmarks to find yourself on the map. You could lose anything out here.

"What's the most important part of the bear fence?" Katmai asked.

I turned to look at him, then glanced down at my sleeves, contemplating whether I had anything unmuddy enough to wipe that big glob of mud off the side of his nose.

"Mom, I *asked* you—What's the most important part of the bear fence?"

"All of it, since we need all the parts to make it work," I answered. "Except the grounding rod, I guess, since we could probably use something else if we lost the grounding rod." And with that, we promptly lost the grounding rod. It was somewhere in Cook Inlet, or perhaps in the MacArthur River, where rippling waves of silt slowly entombed it in the bottom. But the grounding rod is just a piece of metal that can conduct electricity from the wires into the ground.

How would you replace a tent? A pair of pants? A bag of food? The most important part of everything was . . . *everything*. And perhaps the very most important part of that was the packraft. Without a packraft, we couldn't even cross a ten-foot slough. Certainly we couldn't cross bays and rivers and follow the cliffs that lined huge sections of coast. Even a paddle could be improvised.

I'd grown complacent, distracted. I'd been barefoot in the mud, digging with the paddle as the water overtopped each version of our mud-wall dam, and the kids squealed with delighted urgency. "No, Mom, over here! It's leaking over here!" I shoveled a load of dripping goo onto the top of the wall, with the paddle that was no longer attached to the packraft. "We need more on this side!"

The wind took strands of my hair that had escaped my scruffy ponytail and plastered them across my face. "A new channel!" Lituya squealed, and jumped in it, naked from the waist down. I was as engrossed by the play as the kids, but we'd been there a few hours, and it was time to get going. Time to paddle across the brown rush of the MacArthur River and head back in to dry land. I unclipped the drybag from my raft and set it in the bottom of the boat, digging out a diaper for Lituya. Then I sat down beside the remains of our dam, carefully using a sock to wipe all the sand from between my toes. Lituya picked up a handful of sand and tossed it in the air, letting it blow into my face.

"Stop it!" But the sand wasn't what needed to be stopped.

"Get it, Daddy! Get it!" I bolted up at Katmai's scream, shoe dangling from my hand, watching Hig streak past in a dead sprint. Ahead of him, my packraft raced at a similar speed, flipping end over end as it sailed downwind across the flats. Diapers and food spilled out from the bag that used to be inside it.

It hadn't been windy when we got to this spot a couple hours ago. It had only been a little bit windy when I detached the paddle and unclipped the bag. Now it was windy. Hig was sprinting about as fast as the packraft tumbled, but not fast enough to gain any ground. I looked beyond them. It could go at least a dozen miles that direction before it would hit anything solid. Too far to see. Too far to walk today.

"What's going to happen!!?" Katmai was panicked.

"I don't know. Daddy's trying." The packraft paused in its somersault, a stray eddy of air pushing the red balloon against a patch of wet ground. Its back end began to lift, but it was slowed—just barely—by the surface tension of that water. Hig leapt on top of it, tackling the boat with all his weight. I resolved, *again,* to never leave a packraft untethered.

After that, it was hard to feel anything but grateful for the half-hour struggle to paddle across the MacArthur River, inching from sandbar to sandbar against the inexorable force of both current and wind. Thick and brown, the river sprawled across a woven tangle of bars and channels, like most rivers I'd crossed in Alaska. Our rivers are liquefied glaciers. Our glaciers are tongues of ice that have slurped up ancient mountains. The water is wild, pristine, and as dirty as you can imagine.

This place must have been green once. It must have been trees rising from lush swamps, their grasses waving as North America's first voles skittered past. That's the coal in the bluffs. It must have been clear salt water, an ocean filled with tiny cells of algae. That's the oil. Then the ocean and rivers covered them with sand and mud. The glaciers came.

A little more snow fell each winter than the winter before. Each summer, the heat of the sun wasn't quite enough to melt it all. And the glaciers inched forward. The land dropped into an ice age. The glaciers spilled out of the mountains, out of the valleys, out into an ocean that was drying up ahead of them, as more and more of its moisture was locked into the ice. The glaciers filled Cook Inlet with ice, scouring out every fjord and inlet, rolling over all but the mountain tops. They ground it all into dust and spat it out in thick layers that settled to the bottom of the ocean. Glaciers still top our mountains today, still grinding them down, spitting out the silt that eddied in every paddle stroke. The glaciers dug deep, but they couldn't quite dig to the bulk of the oil.

"My favorite is definitely Monopod," I asserted. The oil platform Monopod balanced in the ocean on one squat leg, with three cranes bristling from the top.

"Yeah," Hig agreed. "It has to be Monopod."

The offshore oil platforms were dinosaurs, squatting in the roiling brown water, reaching their necks to the sky. They were steampunk, postapocalyptic constructions set on fat concrete pillars wider than my house. The tide swirled beneath their legs. The gray and yellow beasts grew wider and wider toward the top, their blocky bodies adorned with loops of wire and bristling with odd points, until they were topped by cranes, each sticking off at an improbable angle. Just beyond Monopod, the next oil platform stood on four red legs, a pair of upturned tusks growing from its face, yellow crane antennae cocked to the sound of the sea. That one was named King Salmon. There were more fish names, an Osprey, a Bruce, an Anna, and a few that never got names beyond "A" and "C." They rumbled with a low mechanical drone, and when the first one was half a mile away, Lituya panicked that she was about to get run over by a four-wheeler. At night, we could sometimes see them breathing fire.

The oil platforms *were* dinosaurs. Monopod was erected in 1966. All but one of the sixteen offshore platforms had been built in the 1960s. They've been standing guard over the tides since before I was born. They were here before Prudhoe Bay, before the pipeline, before the words "oil" and "Alaska" became irreversibly linked. Monopod peered over Kenai and Soldotna when only a thousand people lived in what is now an eleven-thousand-person metropolis, before strip malls settled down beside the highway.

Oil is slippery. Hidden. Harder to capture than rock with a pick and shovel. The rocks you live by are important. Thousands of years ago, people sought out the best chert, the best slate, the stones that could be chipped and carved to smooth sharp points. They might have traded the best—the volcanic obsidian from the Alaska Peninsula or the copper from Copper River—with people a thousand miles away. As soon as foreigners set eyes on Alaska, they did much the same. Gold, copper, coal, oil, traded around the world.

The first oil in the state was found on the west side of Cook Inlet in the 1890s, on the Iniskin Peninsula, just a few weeks farther along our route. Back on the east side of the inlet, tucked behind the mudflats of Chickaloon Bay, was the first oil to make anyone any money. The oil pooled beneath both shores—the urbanized east, the remote and unpopulated west—and right down the middle, where the line of the dinosaurs fed beneath the mud and waves.

Swish. Splash. Down one mud bank in a skating wriggle of sneaker prints, starting to rinse off the mud in the knee-deep water just before it was added back to our shoes on the other side. Hig gave Katmai a lift across. It was a break in our plodding stride that was hardly a break in conversation by now, a muddy chasm that was unremarkable in depth, breadth, or foot-sucking power. The final slough of Trading Bay was a plaster on my calves and on the buckles of my pack that were nearly jammed shut with its silt. I squeezed until the buckles finally sprung loose, and disgorged bags and packs and Lituya onto a coal and gravel beach between a pair of driftwood logs.

The spring grass here formed a short, unshaven stubble in the marsh behind us. Violet-green swallows zipped and turned and rested on the sand, pausing in their effort to eat the cloud of crane flies. The rumbling engine startled us all. Not a distant oil platform but a real four-wheeler, pulling up to a stop on the sand beside our fire. A man jumped off. "Hi, I'm Eric." He was forty-something, with a decisive expression, hair shaved close around a shiny bald top. "Eric" was embroidered in white onto the chest of his dark blue Hilcorp shirt.

Lituya clung to my leg, face turned in against the newcomer. Katmai stood next to me, fixing the intruder with a skeptical stare. Eric's hand stretched out toward him then fell, dangling at his side.

"They're a little shy, at first," I offered.

Eric chuckled. "Yeah, I have five kids myself. You must be a good hiker, Katmai. I brought your food, in case you needed it." He gestured at the cardboard box in the four-wheeler's basket.

"Thanks. We just got here . . . ," I began, marveling at the timing.

"I know. We've been watching you on the tracker, and I wasn't sure if you'd need this right away. Or I could take it back to the facility."

Of course. I hadn't exactly forgotten the tracker. It was a black and yellow box I dutifully turned on every day, checking its battery levels, then pushing the button that sent little pieces of data pinging to distant satellites, to be gathered up by a California data center and added to the world's collective public knowledge base. I hadn't forgotten it, but I hadn't quite appreciated how public we really were, even way out here. In a maze of tidal channels, or out on the flats five miles from the closest landmark, I might not know exactly where we were. But anyone else could see. Watching a map on their computer screen, one more blue point appearing every ten minutes. If anyone cared, they could look up how early we rose and how long we stopped for lunch. They might know how fast those currents had really carried us.

We made a plan with Eric to meet up the next day at the Trading Bay Production Facility. Someone would escort us in at 11:30 a.m. at the plant's entrance. We'd pick up the food then, because even a few more miles without that weight was a few more miles of bliss.

Usually the bears walk the coast this time of year, Eric had told us. But the sun hadn't yet beat back the late spring, and only fox or coyote tracks wound between smooth brown whelk shells—themselves the only signs of intertidal life. We strung up the bear fence anyhow, a handy chunk of rusted metal plunged in as our grounding rod.

The next morning, we hiked to the plant's entrance on a wide swath of dirt, neatly packed by the treads of dozers and the tires of large trucks. A new green sign and a rumbling power shovel announced the entrance to the restricted facility. A hard-hatted man jumped out, motor still running, giving us an enthusiastic greeting beside his towering machine. Now this was something a four-year-old boy could get behind. Ice cream in the mess hall, even more so. A dozen or so guys rotated through on their half-hour lunch breaks, staggered from 11:30 to 12:30, work shirt cuffs rolled up above their elbows, pizza and salad and paper cups of soda consumed with the everyday efficiency of people on the clock. Chocolate ice cream spotted Lituya's muddy sun-blocked cheeks like face paint and dribbled down the sides of her cone. It puddled on the table. A large computer screen on one wall of the oil camp lunchroom showed inscrutable numbers and readouts for important equipment somewhere in this city of machinery. An alarm sounded, and Eric ran off.

Trading Bay Production Facility looks like a small city of buildings and tanks and flaring gas. It has been sucking oil from the platforms for more than forty-five years. But the sign was new and the uniforms were fresh, and the latest owners had come in to rework old wells with old workers. Eric had told us it was boom times again, and he should know. Born in Kenai, he'd looked out over those platforms for decades. Now he was forty-three, looking at them from the other side. He spent thirteen years on the Monopod—our favorite silhouette—and worked his way up. One man we'd met in Port Graham had described those platform jobs: each room a metal box that sweated in the heat, echoed with a metallic ring, and felt a little like a prison. But the money was good. Eric didn't complain about any of it. The guys at Trading Bay looked happy. It was easy to see that this was the plum job of the Cook Inlet oil industry, grounded on land you could reach and explore.

The lunchroom wall boasted a plaque from the silver salmon derby the workers organized each year in the nearby Kustatan River. On our way out, we chatted with a guy on break, filling a paper soda cup with pebbles for his rock polisher and fish tank.

Camp jobs are measured in weeks. Here, it's one week on, one week off, half the guys on day crew and half on the night.

You fly back home to Kenai when you're not working. I looked at my messy loud kids with a nervous trepidation. What could they destroy here? Who could they bother? The guys looked at them a little wistfully, squeaky little reminders of home.

Our home in Seldovia is farther away than most of theirs—in straight-line miles as well as in the months stretching ahead before we'd be there. We have fewer creature comforts than the oil guys, and we eat less fresh food than the explorers did. We are never locals—only knowing each place for the time it takes to walk across it. But we've got something they don't. We've got something the oil workers, the explorers, the prospectors and trappers and all the other adventurers and transients of the world almost never have: Family.

People wonder sometimes how we do this with little kids. I wonder, every time I read two-hundred-year-old stories of sailing captains, or modern tales of hard-core mountaineers, how other people do it *without* little kids. When the captain pens terse grumpy logs about the bleak and barren shores, or when a climber or paddler builds a caricature of nature all tooth and claw and vengeful misery to pit himself against, I wonder if he's just homesick. Maybe the struggle and adversity of the adventure has to be played up, to lend weight and worth—to make up for what was left behind.

Family is home. The bedtime ritual of tent staked, sleeping pads inflated, all of us laid out close enough to touch and all the wiggles and stories and "When is it morning time?" All the familiarity and love in the word "home" wrapped up in colorful nylon. I can get cold or wet. I can miss showers and pizza. But I can't get homesick—not for a month, a year, whatever. The most important parts of home are always beside me.

"My shoe!" Hig yelped.

"What?!" I yelled back. Lituya leaned over the edge of the packraft, reaching her fingers into the water. I extracted my foot from knee-deep sand and ankle-deep water, giving the raft another tug. It had to be deep enough to paddle somewhere.

Hig stood on one foot, lifting the other. His sole flapped down, folded until the toe touched the heel, torn all the way across. "Can it wait until camp?"

"It'll have to." He took off both shoes, threw them in the raft, and walked barefoot in the glacial river. The sandbars in the Drift River were new and unsettled, and they tugged at our feet as we waded, plunging and pulling and floating and scraping the bottom of the raft against the sand, trying to get to the ocean.

Redoubt Volcano squats above the wide braided plain of the Drift River, which noses up against the Drift River Oil Terminal. Oil from the Trading Bay Production Facility flows here, beneath the ground we walked and paddled, ready to ship to places beyond. It was built, like most of these facilities, in the 1960s, when the volcano burbled and spit and set loose mudflows (known as lahars) that almost buried the terminal before it was built. Since then, it has been almost buried two more times. In 1990 lahars flooded buildings and damaged the power generation system. In 2009 lahars inched over the berms that guarded the oil tanks, held back only by the snow that topped the berms. No oil was spilled, but you might credit luck as much as any engineering. The volcano is still active and has the potential to release a lahar ten times as large as what those tanks have seen. What happens next time?

The whole industry can seem that way. Massive yet vulnerable. Taxes on oil fund more than 90 percent of Alaska's state government, and the intricacies of those taxes fill newspapers with heated debate. Everyone has reason to care. Every resident, including our children, gets a thousand or two thousand dollars of oil money each year, dividends from the state's Permanent Fund. Oil prices rise, oil prices fall. Surpluses of billions are followed, within a few years, by shortfalls of billions. Legislators argue over what should be cut. The dividend checks, the snowplows, the teachers. Alaskans' dependence seems inevitable, but Prudhoe Bay crude has been flowing for fewer than forty years. The economy of sea otter skins must once have seemed as certain.

Finally, the sand dropped away. Our packrafts floated toward our next stop, and toward the mouth of the inlet. The tide pulled us along, past concrete posts and the wing-like bridges that arched between them. We could see our speed in the current that swirled past the oil terminal's pillars, a spaceship–like creation, currently empty of humans. Maybe every twenty seconds, it blew a foghorn into the sunny evening, alerting the world to its continuous and hulking presence. The oil industry speaks, "I'm still here! I'm still here! I'm still big!"

Puffins wheel around a skiff, as Jon heads out to work on his setnet sites.

FISH CAMP

JUNE 7-12: DRIFT RIVER TO CHISIK ISLAND

"Isn't this what balm of Gilead is supposed to be?" I asked, rubbing a cottonwood bud between my fingers.

"Beats me," Hig replied.

Fat and brown, the new buds looked like scaly bugs and filled the world with a sticky sweetness. It was hot enough, this afternoon, that we wanted the shade of those heart-shaped new leaves that cascaded over the beach. Hig sat barefoot, sewing his shoe back together. The kids squealed, dumping pots full of water on each other at the tiny creek. A family beach vacation. I don't usually call our journeys "vacations." Mostly because vacations are supposed to be easy. Relaxation, hedonistic pleasure, and toothy-grinned snapshots posed with your back turned toward the thing you're supposed to be looking at.

An "expedition"—well, maybe that's supposed to be miserable. The word carries an air of honorable suffering, a whiff of ancient importance that clings from the days when the world depended on explorers. An expedition is ambitious, driven, and all-consuming. How could an eight-hundred-mile journey through sleet and mud under a backbreaking load be anything else?

It is, though. That's why we keep doing it. In our family an "expedition" is any human-powered wilderness journey of a month or longer. This was Lituya's second expedition, Katmai's third, and my sixth with Hig. Expeditions aren't the mountains climbed, the waves paddled, the miles walked, or the storms endured. Expeditions are anything that gives us the time to get into the rhythm of a life outdoors. Until all the rest of your life falls away, and you can hardly remember anything different.

It's just life, and life is not a vacation. Except at the moments when it is. When it's just sun and sticky-sweet air. Just giddy kid laughter and sorting through a pocketful of pumice for the prettiest pebbles, a vacation not from ordinary life but from the unordinary challenges that make up *our* life. Nature has a seemingly infinite capacity to be a hard place for humans, but it can also be easy—easier than any world humans build for themselves. Easy. Beautiful. Amazing.

Smash! Katmai threw a rock as hard as he could manage. I threw a larger one. They each met the boulder with a clattering shatter of shale and sandstone, splitting into sharp-edged plates. Our dusty fingers scraped in the fragments. "Look at this!" he called.

To me, the fossil was indistinguishable from the alder leaves that still littered the beach from last fall's shedding, a brown veiny oval with a toothy edge, pressed into the sand around thirty million years back. The conifers were different—the needles of the ancient metasequoia rounder and stubbier than the modern Sitka spruce, forming black feathery sprays across the reddish stone. Each smash cracked open on a new layer of life—leaves, seeds, cones, and fragments of wood, layered over and over each other in a washed-over jumble like you'd see at the edge of any stream.

The fossils were all too big to carry. I photographed the best ones, then propped them up on top of the sandstone boulders because I thought there might be another human walking by before too long—someone to appreciate what we'd found. This coast was a fish camp place. In Tyonek we'd camped at the Standifers' fish camp. We'd filled our water bottles at Alex and Abby's fish camp before setting out across the Trading Bay mudflats. As soon as we'd left the oil facility, we camped out at a fish camp on the other side. The morning after that we'd walked down the beach, waving to a skiff full of net-picking fishermen in orange gloves and small waves. Before the Drift River tore open Hig's shoe, we'd chatted between bites of cinnamon rolls and Skittles on the porch of a fish camp cabin.

All of these places—the subsistence fish camps in Tyonek and the commercial versions farther on—were setnet sites. Setnetting is a particular form of fishing that balances between the history of fish traps and the commercial fishing boats you might imagine. Nets are anchored to the shore on one end, and the fish are captured as they swim along the coast, headed for their respective streams. The fishermen can live onshore, but they must stay near, close enough to make the rounds of each net in a skiff, setting, picking, and pulling them at the times designated by the government and the tides.

The high tide pushed us up to the crowded edges of the beach, climbing over masses of roots and branches peeled shiny white by the waves. "We'll take a break up at that creek," I told the kids. "By that house."

"Do we get to go in the house?" Katmai asked.

"I don't know. But we can eat our snacks and play."

A man strode down to the beach and stuck out his hand. Wearing XtraTuf boots and a wool hat pulled down over his ears, Don had a wiry gray beard and a face lined from decades of life outside. Upon his invitation, the kids scurried through the beach grass, then through Don's greenhouse crawling with tomato plants, beneath a mobile of beach rocks in shapes so odd you wouldn't believe they were real. Stairs rose from the greenhouse to the house, where I ran my hand over the satiny posts of twisted willow and the coarse fur of a bear skin sprawled over the couch. I cringed as Katmai asked his all-important question: "What can I eat?"

"We just ate lunch," I answered lamely, as the kids proceeded to mooch juice and sandwiches, and I hovered over the shiny floors with a napkin. Some fish camps are shacks. This one was a palace. Don and Ann had been fishing here for longer than I'd been alive, and their summer life paraded across a stretch of coastline as a scatter of green-roofed buildings; their paths and gardens lined with wave-sculpted wood and an ocean of beach treasures.

Fishing was a flurry of fast-paced work, interrupted by long stretches of waiting, repairing, building, and puttering. The next day wasn't a fishing opener. We walked the beach with Don and Ann, and with Don's brother and sister-in-law and a pile of dogs. Shotguns hung from both men's backs. Sun chased the dropping tide, setting steam billowing off the boulder-speckled sand flats. One of the dogs dropped a freshly dug razor clam in front of her owner, who was combing the drift line for anything the waves had brought in. We roasted the clam and the hot dogs over a beach fire. Ann called it "Hawaii," waving her arms to encompass a stretch of beach well-known and loved, the source of endless treasures. How could you imagine people weren't falling over themselves to live this way?

"The reason I came here," Don said, "is the spirit of Alaska— that homesteader mentality. And seeing that degrade . . . You expect it on the road system, but if it starts disappearing in the rural areas too, then we'll be just like everywhere else. And I hope that doesn't happen. I don't see many younger people doing things like we do." He looked over at Lituya, who was scratching lines in the sand with a stick, a half-eaten hot dog dangling from her other hand. "I guess you guys give me hope."

Nearly forty years before we walked along this shore, writer Nancy Lord began netting fish here. Decades ago, she wrote about the dwindling group of commercial fishermen on the west side of Cook Inlet. About how economics and biology and conflicts with sport fishermen had left fewer and fewer people out each summer, running their commercial setnetting operations along the Kustatan Peninsula, just beyond the Trading Bay oil facility. She herself didn't do it anymore. Fewer people were living at fish camps. Fewer people pounding a stretch of beach into their souls, living by the strain of their muscles, the vagaries of fish runs, and the mercy of the tides.

Maybe the world is moving on from family fishing businesses like it's moved on from explorers on sailing ships. Their career was like our expedition. An excuse to live wild and bold, while we still can. We may have given Don hope, but we weren't the same. We moved past. Camped on an alder-draped beach we'd never seen before, eating the salmon fillets we'd been given. Our tent would never wear into a silvery lichen-covered wood, would instead spend its life jumping hundreds or thousands of miles as a garishly out-of-place triangle, and never crumble back into the ground. Our tent was YELLOW!

It blinded me. Inside it, I blinked and rubbed my eyes. The nylon walls were like the sun itself, which shone right through them, intensifying in the bubble of fabric. It was hot. Too hot. I put Lituya on my hip and escaped onto the beach's milder weather, where I found Hig. Lituya squatted beside Hig, who was up early and busy boiling water on a driftwood fire, as usual. He sleeps late at home, but out on the land, the desire to get out into the world was strong enough to pull him out there before anyone else. He lured the kids out with breakfast, and me with hot coffee, which he faithfully made for me, every morning, despite the fact that he hates it himself.

I pulled the tent stakes, lifted the whole thing off Katmai's sleeping form, then crumpled it into a ball. I could hardly believe the day was real. Months of cold, shivering sleet, then suddenly a shimmering green and yellow heat. A golden-crowned sparrow sang from the brush: *twee twee twoooo!* It's a transformation so common, so inevitable, yet so astounding. Every single time.

Have you ever really known spring? In my life I've known three springs. Three springs out on the land when it's hard and white and the bears are asleep and you're out there smelling and breathing that air, every minute of every day, and the sleet stings your cheeks and the slush creeps into your shoes, and it's stark and beautiful and horrible too. And then everything breaks loose. Maybe suddenly, maybe in a maddeningly slow back and forth and back and forth, and why is it snowing again? Until the land flushes green and smells of balm of Gilead and dirt, and the northern sun washes across the whole day, even the middle of the night, and every minute of every day is set to the tune of a thousand birds. Maybe it's the only thing, in my life, that's ever been beautiful enough to make me cry.

Beautiful enough to make me cry, but still, try to imagine what it must be like when that spring was the whole world for the people who lived here, and the life that came back was the whole world? It was sustenance. Life itself. Our sustenance? Well, it was potatoes and oatmeal and pineapples, grown in the heat of a distant sun, dried and shipped with oil that grew in an ancient sun. Oil that could have come from Monopod, through the Trading Bay Production Facility, but probably didn't. Potatoes that could have been grown in this dirt, but they weren't.

We swallowed what we could of spring. Fiddleheads uncurled themselves into the morning's instant mashed potatoes, which were flecked brown with the fuzz we'd been too lazy to pick off and green with the wilted leaves of stinging nettles. I scraped up what portion Katmai left behind, savoring the thick green taste on my teeth, and headed for clams.

Razor clam siphons push oblong holes through the surface of the mud, just a little bit more squashed than the round holes that usually house worms. Razor clams are fast. They squirm downward surprisingly quickly for a creature that looks like a disembodied stomach scantily clad in a thin brown shell, bulging obscenely around the fragile edges. I was soon elbow-deep in mud, pinching that fragile shell as gently as I could until the clam wrenched from the mud with an explosive *shhlllllluuuuck!*

Shhlllllluuuuck! I pulled out a clam, swished it in the water, and tucked it into the pot Hig had balanced on the one barnacle-covered rock the glaciers had seen fit to leave in these mudflats. "You know, we have to actually be able to eat them all," Hig pointed out. *Shhlllllluuuuck!* I wedged the clam between the others, siphon up. *Shhlllllluuuuck!*

"I don't think that's going to fit in the pot," Katmai frowned. *Shhlllllluuuuck!*

"The clam is squirting me!" Lituya squealed, picking up the clam I'd left on the rock, feeling its jet against her sunblock-smeared forehead.

"I'm almost done," I reassured them. "Just a few more holes over here I want to check." *Shhlllllluuuuck! Shhlllllluuuuck!* How could I stop when they were everywhere?

The clams clacked against each other in a giant plastic bag, a suitcase-sized Ziploc. It sloshed heavily, dragging my arms down the quarter mile to the nearest stream. The kids jostled to watch the shells swing open in the boiling water, each wanting to be the first to grasp hold of a slippery brown treat. It was hot and dripping. It was a chewy meaty bite of the sea, and the first swallow was exquisite. And the second bite was just as good, and the third, and . . . well, Hig was probably right about stopping sooner, but our stomachs carried us all the way through both batches of boiled clams, long after the kids had wandered off to play. Couldn't waste any.

I blamed dopamine. Dopamine—a small chemical pinging between neurons that drives the brain's reward circuit—is operating on a clam digger as well as on a cocaine addict. The addiction of clams is like the addiction of berries. It's like the addiction of fish, or firewood, which is also the addiction of money or video game currency, or a bucket full of odds and ends you're sure you can make into something you'll someday need. It's not just pleasure. In fact, scientists have found that the drive for rewards can be uncoupled entirely from the hedonistic pleasure of the reward itself. Brain-damaged animals with broken dopamine circuits will starve to death before they're driven to look for food, even as the food itself, placed in the mouth, brings just as much pleasure. My drive to fill every container with clams was exactly the drive of a squirrel caching spruce cones. Just as fundamental. Just as necessary. Humans never would have made it so far if we weren't driven to gather and hoard what is valuable.

"Look! An isopod!" Katmai yelled. He'd pointed them out earlier, but on the way out to the clam flats, I couldn't be bothered to look for anything else. Katmai's tracks stopped at the isopod tracks. This time mine did too. They're also called sea roaches. Dinosaur bugs. *Pentidotea wosnesenskii*. Translucent green or brown as if they were made simply of a hardened version of the seaweeds they eat, arranged into a line of lobster-like segments above skittering legs, behind a pair of wiggling antennae. Hovering, swimming, crawling, the inch-long creatures skated through shallow pools above the mud, headed no particular direction, the edges of their squiggles decorated with the prints of fourteen tiny feet.

I could have watched the isopod for hours. What eats an isopod? How can it find enough seaweed in these muddy waters? How far might a single isopod travel? How long do they live? How many generations of people have eaten clams and fish here? How many have run their hands over the fossils and watched the skittering bugs? This curiosity—the tug of war between the practical and the wonderful—is the essence of being a human. Humans would never have made it so far if we weren't driven by wonder.

We moved on. The Crescent River spit fresh trees into the ocean, tumbling fast and strong and cloudy. The sun floods the glacial rivers, more than rain ever could, the sudden shift in temperature unhinging those stolid icy faces. I ferried hard. Each paddle stroke pulled me a few feet across and several feet downstream. I hopped out on the downstream corner of the first gravel bar, danced a bit to bring the life back to my ice water–chilled feet, and dragged the raft, plus the pack, plus a sleeping Lituya, up to the upstream end. Without my weight, the raft's bow tipped up, hanging in the air as if it wanted to take off. It was heavy, unbalanced, scraping hard against the clattering of gravel. I crossed the next channel, and the next.

There were fish camps near this shore too. I didn't know exactly who they belonged too, and maybe no one else did either, mired in a family feud/legal dispute that we'd somehow inadvertently skated into. One of the family members we'd met in Anchorage offered to bring our food resupply to this spot, but now he'd learned that we had stayed with a friend of the family member on the other side of the dispute and suspected us of ill intentions. His ranting messages scrolled out across the screen of our little satellite communicator, one to two dollars a pop for every 140 characters. But stamping out the fires of perceived injustice did nothing to budge the basic logistics. The guy with our food wasn't here.

We would run out of food, if we stayed at this beach. We could hike to find the people on the other side of this family dispute. We could ration our food. We could eat razor clams until we burst and try not to care about the rest of it. I frowned at the communicator screen.

"Chisik Island?" Hig suggested. Three miles offshore, the island beckoned from the middle of Tuxedni Bay, a slanted prow of land decorated with a few squiggles of snow and a blush of slowly climbing green. There were fishermen there too, we knew, and it was on our route. I blew the last puffs of air into my raft and set it optimistically by the water's edge. The day breeze was up, the three miles quickly filling with chop.

"Not yet," I answered. The chop peaked into scattered whitecaps. The weather was unsettled, shifting. Too much could happen in three miles of paddling. Better to be cautious.

"Where's my long rock?!" Lituya screeched. I scuffed my feet in the sand beside her, handed her a wave-smoothed, hand-oiled stone the size and shape of my middle finger. She clutched it as she'd clutched it for days, the most important object in the world.

Just beyond the edge of the sand, I gathered handfuls of curled yellow-green moss, shaking the spruce needles out, wondering how much I'd need to improvise a few days' worth of diapers. This was the first time I'd needed to try it. Diapers were supposed to be in that resupply. Maps. Maybe other things. Who could remember what seemed so important when we'd packed that box months ago?

Hig turned to set up the tent. Katmai squatted by the fire, tossing in small sticks by the handful. Between the kids and the boats, a family of four river otters scampered past, their long bodies stretching and springing in a sinuous lope. Our rafts sat on the shore, expectant as if we might still jump in, sometime in the middle of the night to paddle across. Maybe we would. The tide should be best at 4 a.m.

We weren't best at 4 a.m. I've read about those paddlers who use midnight tides. The mountaineers who begin climbs at 3 a.m. They have more dedication than I do. The earliest we could peer, bleary-eyed, out of the tent was 6:30 a.m. It was long past sunrise, and my brain sleepily unscrambled the glare on the water into something probably smooth enough to paddle. At least as far as our eyes could resolve it. Which is never quite far enough, so you weave your way out of the shallow flats, eyes on those waves—not whitecapping. Wait, okay, maybe 5 percent whitecaps, not too many. Steep but small, shouldn't be a problem unless the current sets up too strong against them or the wind increases. Feel the gusts, try to compare to half an hour ago, an hour ago, when you were eating breakfast. It's just a stiff breeze. The few rattling gusts tugged at the loose hood of my raincoat, then fell back, not quite mustering the energy to turn into anything more.

None of this would matter except that three miles takes an hour and a half in a packraft. Any oceangoing vessel captain has to think ahead.

Just like in the Crescent River, we pointed our boats at an angle, paddling toward somewhere beyond where we actually meant to go, compensating for the pull of the tide. Chisik Island was getting closer, quickly. Even Lituya barely had time to sleep before we bumped our bows against the gravel shore, right in front of a curious crowd. A woman stepped in front of the group, in blue fishing waders and a baseball cap. "Are you Erin and Hig?"

"Yes." Who was *she*? My mind turned blank. Is this someone I'm supposed to know? Are the people over here on one side or the other of the land feud we're trying to escape?

"Where did you come from?" she asked us.

"Well, we came from a long way away," I started. "Two and a half months ago."

"The tip of the Kenai Peninsula," Hig answered.

They introduced themselves as friends of a good friend from home. Paula, the one who'd greeted us by our names, led us past the trampoline, the picnic table with the purple and blue umbrella, the shed with the basketball hoop, and a pile of plastic water jugs into a small dark cabin wallpapered with books and thick with the smell of fresh bread.

"A vole!" High-pitched squeals rung out from between a pair of buildings. Three children—two twelve-year-old girls and a ten-year-old boy—dashed back and forth around the edges of the shed, their shoes kicking up a tiny dust tornado.

"It went that way!"

"Into the grass!"

"I see it!"

"Got it!"

One of the girls cupped the squirming bundle in two hands, and carefully carried it over to the fish tote, where the vole immediately hid in the hollow of an old paper towel roll. I followed, lifting Lituya up so she could peer over the edge.

"Do you want to hold one?" The girl set a plump short-tailed rodent in Lituya's hands, stroking the brown and white fur with a finger to calm it down. "This is the tamest one."

I never knew voles could be anything but brown. I'd never considered that this ubiquitous garden pest—Alaska's equivalent of a mouse—could be tamed. The girls had names for them all. Each year Jon and Paula's daughter caught voles, fed them and pet them and kept them in a fish tote, then let them all go at the end of the summer. After years of this, the voles on this end of Chisik Island were decidedly friendlier than their wholly wild cousins.

Rodent excitement done, the boy resumed his flips on the trampoline, long blond hair gleaming above the field of lupines and dandelions. Later, I watched all the kids (Paula and Jon's two plus a visiting friend) jump from rock to rock on the beach, hunting for puffin and oystercatcher nests. They looked so easy and comfortable in their world, moving with a grace I couldn't hope to match, loving it still, even at ten and twelve. I watched them closely because I wanted to see what it could be like. I wanted my kids to grow up like that too.

This family lived here, like most of the setnetters, for two months out of every year. Jon's a teacher the rest of the year. In this place, fishing is a teacher's job. On the west side of Cook Inlet, we'd met teacher-fishermen, retired fishermen, and a radiologist fisherman. Professionals with a fishing hobby, all. The setnetters on this side of the inlet couldn't build their life around fish anymore. At least they couldn't build their income around fish, any more than we could build our income around walking down the beach. A life is something different. Paula and Jon had met on Chisik Island, where Paula had been fishing since she was fourteen. Their kids have been fishing here their whole lives.

We stayed on Chisik Island for two days. So we only saw it in the sun—a gleaming green tower of an island, where waterfalls spit at beaches cobbled with the ancient fossils of bivalves and ammonites. A day before their fishing season opened, we rode in their skiff to a tiny nearby island, in a trip to repair net anchors that was mostly a beach picnic. Back at their camp, the biggest project was building a sand castle on a slab of stone. We laid wet newspaper on the sand, daubing clay over the top that liquefied and slumped as we worked—a more perfect version of a preschool craft project—destined to become an outdoor oven.

"I can only live in Homer," Jon said, "because we get to come out here for two months every year, right when everything starts getting crazy." I know, as an adventurer, that you *can* hang a life on the backbone of a few months each year. You *can* hang a culture on the backbone of salmon, on a necklace of chalky vertebrae washed up on the beach like a hundred little beads.

The rhythms of a place shape us. It's easiest to see this when you look back at the cultures that belonged to Cook Inlet for thousands of years. When you look at the Dena'ina here, and the Alutiiq on the inlet's outer edge, whose every word and custom were forged in concert by the people and the land. Salmon returned to the coast each summer, sorting themselves into families at each particular stream. Human families moved with the rhythm of the piscine. The Dena'ina named directions based on the flow of the inlet—upstream and downstream. Old photographs and older drawings show salmon flayed open, hanging on racks beside temporary camps.

I can't pretend to know how much of that has been lost. But I can see that Alaska geography is powerful. It thrusts itself through the habits of newcomers like the mountains thrust up by the crumpling plates. I can see how quickly salmon swim, like errant fish colonizing a new stream, into all of our blood.

Fish camp is Alaska. Bits of it travel the highway in the backs of pickup trucks, in long-handled dipnets and coolers heading for the Kenai River. There are pieces of it in the smokehouses my neighbors put up, in the salty-chewy strips my kids' friends bring on hikes, and in the silver salmon trophy on the oil camp wall. In the chest freezers in the garage that replaced the earthen pits the Dena'ina used to store salmon. There are little pieces of fish camp in the hearts of people from Iowa, Pennsylvania, or Maine.

Fish was a rush of get-rich-quick like gold was. Like oil. In the early 1900s, taxes on fish supplied up to 85 percent of the revenue to run the territory of Alaska. Fish money then was as omnipresent, as important, as oil money is today. Statehood was won on fish—in a battle that pitted local fishermen against Seattle fish trap owners who controlled the runs from afar. But fish was always something more. Most of Alaska's seven hundred thousand people don't depend on our salmon. But we cling to those gleaming silver bodies, the ruby flesh, as if they were the very jewels they mimic. When runs decline, we fight bitterly over who deserves to catch them. Our population churns and tumbles in a flux of bright-eyed newcomers and snow-weary escapees, turning over faster than in any other state. But the salmon still swim, tenaciously, into the heart of Alaska.

In the distance, pinprick silhouettes stand on the only patch of ground above the tide's reach, beneath the cavernous sea arch that sheltered us.

BEAUTIFUL
PRISONS

JUNE 13–23: CHISIK ISLAND TO THE INISKIN PENINSULA

If not mudflats, then cobbles. Boulders. Sculpted sandstone cliffs that curved down smoothly before jutting into the ocean like a middle finger, cutting off our passage. The world has to be built of something, after all. Katmai leaped from boulder to boulder, narrating his efforts in a constant play-by-play. "See how far this boulder is from that roundy one? Watch me jump! I'm a little bit scared, so it might take a while. Did you see that? Did you expect that I could jump so far?"

I picked up Lituya from where she'd wandered down to the bottom of the beach at the end of our break, her cheeks puffed out with mysterious somethings. "Are you eating rocks?"

"No."

"Wood?"

"No."

"Lituya, you have to tell me. *P-too!* Say *P-too!* You can't just eat things that aren't food." But poisonous plants don't grow down at the tide line, or so I told myself as I questioned her with increasing agitation. She opened her mouth in a giant grin, to display two brown curls perched on her tongue. "Snails!!" I winced as she crunched down.

The cobbles were round and gray, and they clattered over each other in the waves. Rock rose and cinquefoil burst out of cracks in the cliffs. The land was green, and we'd seen our first brown bear only the day before. The kids were running around like wild things at 11 p.m., casting long shadows over the beach berm we were camped on. The world, all of it, was awake.

We listened to the surf pound all night, and watched the shore when we woke up, waiting for an opening. When the wind settled, we paddled away around the cliff. But swells outlast the wind. A packrafter's eyes hover just two and a half feet above the water's surface, and three-foot swells rose up to swallow our horizon. Their shining fingers raked the sky. Surf rolled across the shoals, those shining fingers crumbling to white, speckled with the heads of seals that dragged themselves from beach to ocean as we passed. We crawled around them, each paddle stroke barely keeping ahead of the current.

We'd left the fish camps behind, and the inlet grew wider every day, letting in a little more of the ocean's surf with every mile we traveled. In the mudflats we'd take any solid land we could get. Here we needed landings. The surf threatened to roll us against the shore. We'd be fine, but we'd be soaked, and even an Alaska summer isn't warm enough for that. We stayed outside the breaks. The tide sped up and the current was even harder to paddle against. I wished we could land. Maybe we could find a spot in the mouth of the next river, a few miles farther beside the sedge flats.

It took hours. I stumbled onto the sand in small enough waves, dragging the boat above the swash before the curls could crash over Lituya inside it, scanning the shore for moving lumps. Bears graze in sedge flats. The first bear I spotted was far away, heading for the river from the other side. The second one was a sudden crashing in the trees beside the meadow's edge—Hig's quick glimpse of brown. The third was on the trail we walked, passing by unconcernedly as we dodged a quarter mile into the grass. I clutched Katmai's hand as we followed their trail to Silver Salmon Creek Lodge.

The lodge was populated by long snub-nosed camera lenses, colorful coats, and skinny tripod legs. Our kids quickly commandeered the trampoline beside the dining hall. Self-published coffee-table books splayed out across the coffee tables, filled with rollicking cute bear cubs photographed by former guests.

A little later, I stood up in my clean but torn raingear with my clean ponytail frayed out into split ends, with my arm cupped beneath Lituya's freshly diapered bottom as I balanced her on my hip. I talked about the pictures we had taken. I wanted to say "I'm just like you," but I knew it wasn't true. Their bear photos were much better, much closer than I ever wanted mine to be. They were tourists, and I was too, but I was also something different. I wanted them to understand that it wasn't because I was tougher or stronger or poorer or bravely entering into battle with a cruel and callous nature. I'd just decided to swallow such a big piece of the earth that it was stuck in my throat. The waves that we paddled look different when you fly over them. The bears look different when you cluster in tight formation beside an armed guide. I could show them where Cook Inlet was so ground into my skin that no shower could touch it, but I couldn't explain what that meant.

The yard was sunny and dusty, and it smelled like the cranberry twigs my kids snapped and the yarrow they plucked as they crashed through the bushes. I waved at trailers full of photographers and the guides pulling those trailers behind dusty four-wheelers. I watched the lumbering shapes of the bears, which looked from my distance (through my camera lens) like brown shapes only barely distinguishable from cows. It was time to move on. And not just because our packs were full of food and the swells had calmed, and the tide rip everyone had warned us of—the "rhubarb patch" with waves like monstrous heart-shaped leaves—was a ruffle the height of a chubby toddler fist. It was because my mother was coming, and we wanted to meet her.

Hig shimmied up a spruce to hang our food in a tree by Spring Point Lake. I took the paddle that wasn't holding up our tent and piled shovelful after shovelful of gravel on the bug netting that hung down from its lower edge like a wispy gray skirt. Gravel—precariously balanced on that flat-topped blade—cascaded on my shoes, back into the pile I scraped it from, and in a crunching dribble all the way to the pile where I was putting it. The tent had no floor and a broken zipper, and though we'd hung the same fringe of netting hopefully on the last several incarnations of the tent, it almost never worked. At least, due to a lucky quirk of genetics, I am immune to mosquito bites.

But we'd be sitting an extra day, so maybe camp was worth an extra half hour's work. An expedition is a punctuated experience. It's a rhythmic weaving in and out of humanity's world, and each time we connect it's like Christmas—or maybe like the long-ago Christmas stories where a kid could be excited by a single orange. Carried by Grandma!

I call my mother Niki, which is what most everyone else calls her too. The kids call her Nin. When the floatplane that carried her touched down on Spring Point Lake, she hadn't just brought oranges but also grapes, radishes from the garden I was missing at home, canned salmon and hard-boiled eggs, and a pair of plastic dinosaurs, one for each child. Niki claims she's not an adventurer. "Not like you guys." Just a nearly sixty-year-old woman who will leap into the wilderness with a towering backpack, a tiny raft, and an intention to hike and paddle these bear-strewn shores with us for a month, or as long as it takes.

Maybe, you think, she just didn't know what she was getting into. Someone should have found her in Europe or in South America, left a note on her camper van at a desert trailhead; someone should have warned Niki that her daughter's plan was crazy. But she knew that already. This wasn't her first expedition with us, and it wouldn't be her last. I come by crazy honestly.

"You told me to bring sunblock," Niki reminded me. I shrugged. Rain beaded up on the oily coat of sunblock on Lituya's face. It dripped off her hood, down onto the once bright life vest, to add to the puddle in the bottom of the packraft that might, eventually, reach up to my butt. If it did, it would meet the water creeping down from above, pooling from my wrists to my elbows, pattering against my thighs and running down the length of my raincoat to soak my crotch. It was warm rain, and it jiggled the bay into ripples.

The last time I took a long paddle trip with my mother, it was ninety degrees in a rainforest. How much luck can you ask for? That was nine years earlier. I inherited my adventurousness from her, as well as my natural pessimism, so it was only natural that we found ourselves—me in my twenties and Niki in her fifties then—so convinced that our three weeks in Southeast Alaska would be a deluge of rain that we had absolutely nothing to wear for the hot sun we encountered.

On that expedition, she was the expert kayaker between the two of us, and I had borrowed one of her kayaks for our several-hundred-mile circumnavigation. I was the one infatuated with the Alaskan wilderness, and I bushwhacked my way up a forest and muskeg mountain while she stayed at the beach to wash her hair. She knew, by then, not to follow me into the brush. I'd already quit graduate school while Hig was still grinding through his PhD, but Niki was in the middle of one of her many temporary retirements and had evidently forgiven me for the Alaska trip a few years previous where she'd sprained both her ankles and I'd brought nothing to eat but Nutella and homemade cookies. Needless to say, we had quite a history.

Even warm rain gets chilly in the space of three miles, all sprawled out in a packraft with so much of yourself exposed. I clenched and unclenched my fists around the paddle, willing my fingers to warm. Oystercatchers squealed at the edge of the tide line. Puffins dove from the cliffs, their fat bodies swooping so low in a whoosh of frantic wingbeats that it looked like they would crash before they flew. Then one did. A plummeting plop. Grace in the water and awkward competence in the air. I envied both qualities.

We were on the Iniskin Peninsula. The layered cliffs of the Tilted Hills stacked up like leaning sheets of plywood. Waterfalls played with them. Waves punched arches through the layers like hopped-up martial artists. Waves scratched out deep caves with their slippery strong fingers. Waves threw stones at the cliffs, leaving the rubble of their games piled beside them.

I was offshore, watching Niki poised on the boulders, waiting for just the right moment to launch. She shoved the boat into the water, knee-deep herself, then jumped in, paddles whirling against the swashes of white. "So?" I asked when she rejoined me.

"I don't think we could camp on those boulders," she said.

I nodded. It hadn't looked likely. "Thanks for being the scout." As slowly as I could manage, I shoved my feet along the taut rubber of the raft tube, tightening one cramped knee and bending the other from its overstretched position. Lituya was heavy in her sleep, propped up on my lap above the errant wave that had leapt into the boat when I'd launched it.

They were three foot seas—or less. I'm sure they were less, but it didn't matter on the beach that morning, when I set the raft on the boulders as close as I could to the waves and buckled the pack on and lifted Lituya in and tried to push it far enough beyond the surf zone that I could clamber in and . . . We each tried once and failed, emptied boats full of water, unloaded pissed-off kids back onshore, and tried again. The second try smacked us with a second wave, but I didn't care: I just wanted to be out there.

Fighting the wind along the cliffs, even with a favorable current, was slow and sloppy. It was only early afternoon, and this was the second hopeful camp that Niki had scouted. Nothing looked good. Everything looked gorgeous. The tilted cliffs were conglomerate—a matrix of gray stubbled with cobbles and pebbles that felt, under your hand, like the worn-down surface of a cobblestone road. Waterfalls shredded into a million strands around each dark lump. The lighter lumps were seals, and some of them simply rolled off the cliffs as we approached. A dozen heads, dark wet gray now, periscoped up as we paddled toward their cave.

They watched us enter. Wind blew through the dark tunnel. It was the largest sea cave I'd ever seen. Seal bellies had left furrowed tracks in the gravel and, back in the dim depths, a skeleton of seal bones slowly fell apart into tendon-joined white. Our voices echoed in a space that smelled of seal crap and fish, of rot and salty decay.

Later that day, we encountered a second cave. "I bet you could fly a plane through this," Hig marveled. "Not that I'd want to be on it."

I craned my head back to examine the top of the arch. While the first cave had been fit for a haunted house, this one was an airy cathedral. A vaulted roof led down to a broad pillar of rock that could have been an island itself, each side of the arch a window to the waves.

"Are you sure this is high enough above the tide?" Niki asked. She was standing on the gravel beach beneath the arched roof, which was the only remotely flat dry piece of land we'd seen all day, excepting the graveyard of seals.

"No." I paced the line of kelp, tracing the curve with the remains of my sneakers. I paused at the highest cusp of a wave-tossed blade, laid my head on the gravel, and squinted up at her knees. "But I think we're okay. It's 18.9 at 12:43 in the morning and it was 17.6 last night." I had checked the crumpled tide book page at least three times already. I'd memorized the numbers but pulled it out again and read them off directly. I glanced above the gravel beach, to the sandstone ledges that stair-stepped up above it, imagining a groggy scramble, sleeping bags and tents tossed up to crouch above the waves, watching the ocean wash through below us. But what other spot would we find? What other prison could be so beautiful?

At 11:30 p.m. I flicked on my headlamp to write by. It wasn't dark outside yet, but it was dark beneath our stone roof. Hig was telling a bedtime story about talking ravens and time-traveling soldiers, and I almost couldn't hear him because the waves were so loud. So close. The cobbles clattered. I peered out the two-inch gap we'd left beneath the walls of the tent, looking at the approaching ocean. A little over an hour to high tide. Hig's story wound down into a mumbling sleepy ending. Lituya shot out her hand, grabbed a chunk of granite to snuggle up with. My pencil scratched faster now that everyone was quiet.

I woke up from a fitful doze an hour or two later, and peering into the blue gloom, it was clear the water was retreating. The 12:43 a.m. high tide had passed. I nudged Hig in the bag beside me. "Happy tenth anniversary!"

We had taken our wedding vows on summer solstice, in a Seattle park, where friends sang, other friends brought homemade carrot cake and grilled fish, a friend joined a ministry on the internet in order to marry us, and we paddled away into the evening in a pair of brand-new packrafts my father had given us.

"Happy anniversary," he replied. "I love you."

"I love you too."

When we woke up later that morning, we'd share a bit of chocolate. Not too much. You have to eat sparingly when you're stuck. If we'd been in Seldovia, we would have thrown a great solstice party. Salmon and pies and just-picked radishes and dogs snatching food off the plates of toddlers, and all of us scuffing our feet on the gravel driveway in idle chatter until the mosquitoes came out and the sun finally set around midnight, just north of the peak of Mount Iliamna. Mount Iliamna was behind us now. Twenty miles north instead of sixty miles across Cook Inlet, completely obscured by our stone roof stretching across the sky and the hulking mass of the Iniskin Peninsula, which we never even notice, looking across from home. At that distance, the lower mountains are just an unremarkable haze. Obstacles usually are, at a distance.

Before I closed my eyes that night, I had peered out under the edge of the tent again. The waves never reached the berm that protected us, but even in the 2 a.m. dimming, I could tell they would never let us launch. So I slept in, curled up with Lituya against the wind rushing in through the gap.

At breakfast, we huddled around the fire, plotting our escape. Hig had tried to scale the slopes, and he told us that the roof of our arch was flat marsh and wildflowers, but probably nothing we could climb, with the kids. The tide had risen over the flat reefs and was creeping up the gravel. By afternoon, our arch would be a portal to nothing, open on both sides to the jumbled reflection where waves jostled waves until they grew irritated with their crowds and lashed out in crashing white spikes that frothed the ocean. Sea spray blew across our spit, and at high tide the two sides of the ocean almost met.

We were stuck here because it happened to be bad paddling weather, which was common, and the shores were lined by cliffs, which was common, and because those crumbling cliffs left no beaches beneath them, which wasn't common at all. A flat rocky reef fringed all of these cliffs, and you could walk on the mussels and anemones, just until the tide rose back above zero. Tonight was due to be the full moon and second-highest tide of the month, at 21.1 feet. Tomorrow would be the highest, at more than 22 feet. Our survey of the tide line was twice as deliberate as it had been the day before—and three times as anxious. We had no level, but we had paddles and string and we tried to survey the land as best we could. Our tents would stay dry in their spot for one more night, assuming the tide came exactly as forecast, but not two.

We had twenty-four hours to escape.

Twenty-four hours, and nothing we could do right now but wait for conditions to change. Katmai ran down to the waves with his hooked stick, running back to the fire with an imaginary catch of salmon or octopus, leaving dripping wet ovals of feet on gravel.

Lituya picked up colorful pebbles, feeding us our medicine in measured handfuls. I tossed them over my shoulder and pretended to swallow.

They were growing up out here, in rubber raingear and wet salt air. Katmai was growing up to be utterly immune to physical discomfort, just like his dad. He was growing up to be an incorrigible geek and incessant chatterbox, a dimple-crinkled smile beneath hair streaked blond by the sun. Lituya was a sturdy snuggly body beneath chocolate and mud-streaked freckles. She didn't eat sand by the fistful anymore, but I bet she had eaten gallons of it anyway, across the months of our journey. She was too young to remember this. Maybe they both were.

I had grown up here too. I didn't eat as much sand as they did, but I'm sure I ate some. I was twenty-one and just out of college, and I see now why the pilot balked at dropping off two brand-new grownups just up the Drift River valley from the oil terminal, up the coast from where we were now. "Don't pick us up," we'd said. "We're walking to Chignik." Over the next two months, Hig and I did walk to Chignik—our first eight-hundred-mile expedition. We survived our green tarp and lack of proper sleeping bags, our balloon-strength rafts and horribly short food calculations, the bears and the storms and the thickets of devil's club. We survived each other too, in a thin fleece sleeping bag that barely fit our two bodies folded into a single shape. The people we met on that journey seemed more impressed by that than anything.

"I think I can glue a Ziploc bag in there. I bet that might be just enough thickness to counteract what's been lost with those worn-out threads." Hig was our repair guy, dedicated sewer and gluer whose tendency to reinvent the wheel with every project was an asset out here—when we had to make do with whatever tools were handy.

"And if it isn't? How can we really trust it?" My job was to run through the "what-ifs"—to make a Plan B and C and D in case Hig's hopeful Plan A fell short. In case the packraft seemed likely to deflate all of a sudden in the waves.

"We can glue the valve shut, if we really have to." The yellow packraft hadn't been with us on that first eight-hundred-mile voyage. But it had traveled well over four thousand miles, from Seattle to the Aleutian Islands. Each time we blew it up, microscopic particles of plastic rubbed off the screw threads of the valve, scattering themselves across thousands of miles of beaches and river bars. Yesterday I'd pulled it up beneath our sea arch. It hissed and sputtered with the sudden pressure of a bump on a rock. Each time I turned the valve, it popped back out again, until I lifted that sad floppy piece of yellow, imagining a yelling soaking midwater rescue into the other two boats.

You can fudge nearly everything, to some extent. A tent by huddling under a tree or in a cave, insulation by stuffing grass in your hat, food by wading into a salmon stream with a tangled bit of net or remembering that it takes several weeks to starve for real. But you can't fudge flotation.

In 1910, in the middle of January's ice, the steamship *Farallon* hit one of those flat reefs that lines this coast. Ice floes crunched past its hull, and blowing snow blotted out the land. All they had wanted was to drop a pair of men off at that godforsaken portage to Iliamna Lake, but they all ended up on the shore. Thirty-two people ate raw bacon and bread in the almost-always dark, for a month, until they were rescued. Except for the "brave six" who set out to paddle to Kodiak, first to Cape Douglas, as far as we were going, and then even farther, across Shelikoff Strait, thirty miles we'd never dare to paddle. They set out in a lifeboat that was crushed in the ice within days, suffered frostbite and hypothermia, got help, nearly starved, wrecked another boat, and finally borrowed a leaking dory that delivered them to Kodiak, nearly two months later. People had been looking for them for a month already.

We had half a day left before our arch flooded, and we wouldn't make it far without a boat. We had to escape. I left Hig to finish this repair, like all gear repairs, while I went to calculate our food allowance for this day of being stuck, like all the food allowances for all the days of being stuck. We call it "division of labor," and it is, but the truth is that both of us grew up here. I met Hig when I was eighteen, and maybe you could say I've accomplished a lot since then, and maybe you could say that on my own, I've never accomplished anything at all. We are a team. We grew up on expeditions—together.

Six-thirty a.m. with the tide. Okay. Even I can do early, if the alternative is sleeping in the ocean. Niki's phone alarm beeped. She woke us with a hushed voice, and we packed with the same, trying to preserve the kids' sleep as long as possible. Low tide opened up the world. The rounded boulders at the top of the beach led down to a low flat shelf, stretching off into the infinity of minus 4 feet, furrowed as if a plow had raked it, with anemones in every crevice and huge limpets on the upper surface, eating the smear of seaweed that coated the rocks.

"You said we'd go low-tiding," Katmai complained, once we were finally on our way. Didn't we know that meant a leisurely lifting of seaweed fronds, not this tugging held-hand hurry? I pointed out anemones. A few hermit crabs. If we let the tide rise now, we had literally nowhere to go. We had to escape. Hurry.

Across a creek that sprawled shallowly across the low-tide boulders—long enough that the initial shock of feet-plunged-in-ice was followed by a needling pain of cold. Around the sandstone ridges that jutted into the seaweed, and the scattered pocket beaches that wouldn't last more than a few hours as the tide rose, until we reached a stream that spattered through a gully you could follow above the tide. I walked up it. Lituya did too, while she played "four-wheeler takes sick people to the hospital" on a log beside the spindly twigs of heather. I walked farther, into the depths of a forest laced with towering devil's club plants, that had me crawling over and under everything just to get a few hundred yards. There was no way through that I could see between the branches.

We had escaped. And we were stuck again. We were safe from the rising tide, but it was the ocean or nothing going forward.

So we built a fire to cook a meal of instant potatoes, with red-stemmed petrushki (lovage) plucked from the upper edge of the beach, and fat limpets plucked from the bottom edge, and we watched the waves. It implies a contemplative sort of thing, watching the waves. The wilderness shore as a Zen-like place of dreamy purity. The truth is that the ocean is loud. And watching the waves is not at all like daydreaming. You can spend hours shouting over their din, discussing the intricate dance between specific curls and specific boulders, solving a problem with no clear answer.

"It's bigger surf than we've launched into before," I said.

"It's more than I would do in my kayak," Niki said.

"It's really nice beyond the break," Hig said. "Flat calm out there. And there ought to be less swell on the dropping tide."

"Let's watch it," I finished.

We moved the fire out of the drizzle under a dry cliff overhang, where the smoke curled against the cliff and rose straight up like it was a chimney. Each adult took it in turns to stand at the edge of the waves, weighing our options. It's important, as an adventurer, to have a vividly pessimistic imagination. You might skip visualizing the sudden meteor impact or unpredicted volcanic eruption, but most regular disasters should be thoroughly imagined before they occur. So your dry bags are closed up and thrown to the top edge of the tent before you sleep, and you've certainly imagined falling off that cliff before you step anywhere near it. Because the point is to steer clear of any of those pessimistic imaginings that involve death or significant injury.

After hours of pessimistic imagining, the launch was like a spell of déjà vu. I dragged my boat over the slick round boulders just as a smaller-than-average wave crashed against them. I got off easy. I paddled ashore again for Hig to drop Lituya onto my lap, and a wave left me stranded on a rock, just about to be swamped by the next wave crashing into shore when Hig managed to shove me out beyond it, six inches to spare.

Niki was next. She dragged her boat over the slick round boulders, poised to get in and then the wave crashed down. It was too big to even stand up against, and it swashed her and the boat in its foaming pools, sending her scrambling to grab and dump the boat—raingear plastered wet against her body. She was luckier the second time out. Hig dropped Katmai into her boat in the same way he'd dropped Lituya into mine. That part went well.

Hig was last. He was stronger than either of us, and more experienced, and he didn't have a kid to wrangle, but he didn't have luck either. He launched. A wave broke beneath his bow, raising the bottom of the raft until it tilted and toppled and he slipped out into the ocean, swimming back to shore, to try again, killing the helmet cam in the video he was taking along the way. Farther out, the four of us ate potato chips in the calm and watched him suffer.

Soaked, check. Awkward, check. Nonessential piece of gear killed, check. Bodies and spirits, just fine. Kids, bubbly and crunching those potato chips. Beyond the first few feet, the water was beautiful. Huge smooth swells rose and fell under our boats. Flocks of murres flickered as they appeared and disappeared behind the waves, flying just above the surface. Waves crashed on cliffs, then on the low-tide bedrock. But we were outside it all, spinning our arms for nine continuous miles of joyful movement, which was also nine continuous miles of no great landings, so we might as well enjoy it—being stuck in the sea for a change.

Surf broke in rolling lines across the sand flats of Oil Bay. But it was small surf. Sand was not boulders. Our standards were low. We paddled for shore. Landed, this time, far less eventfully than we had launched. We were three generations around a campfire, popping popcorn and passing around M&Ms, drying our soaking clothes, and laughing at the antics of the children. A little after midnight, we crawled into bed in the woods, the kids all amped up from their naps in the boats (or was it the M&Ms for dinner?) and the rest of us adults exhausted. We were stuck again. I looked out at the waves and tried to stare at them, tried to forget for the moment that we'd need to figure out how to launch out past them again in the morning.

I took a moment to love this beautiful prison.

A brown bear mother and her cub run along the shore, hurrying past our lunch spot.

A WORLD BUILT OF BEARS

JUNE 24–JULY 5: INISKIN PENINSULA TO McNEIL HEAD

Seaweed steamed. Sun broke through the clouds and sent misty wisps rising from every strand of ribbon kelp as I stumbled and slid over the world's hidden lumps. I tried to hold Lituya's hand, though I was falling down pretty much as often as she was. The tide was a minus 5.8, and if you've spent any time around tides, you'll know that the tide books print negative numbers in a special bright green color. Zero is "mean lower low water" and on average that's as low as it gets. If the book reads minus 5.8, it means that I could stand at the water's edge, and know that the usual day's beaches are well above my head. It's the closest you can get, without scuba gear, to standing at the bottom of the ocean.

Brittle stars waved impossibly thin arms above the pink-striped shells of chitons. We poked squishy sponges and slimy-stiff tunicates and the rough crusts of bryozoans. Helmet crabs scuttled back into seaweed hidey holes. I tried not to dip my camera in the salt, and I prodded, poked, squealed, and pretended it was all for the children. This tiny island was named Scott. In the catalog of white-person names that overprint the originals, surnames are common. Other common categories include permanently enshrined complaints (Difficult Creek, Dangerous Cape) or obvious wildlife observations. We'd passed both a Gull Island and a White Gull Island in the past week and were hurtling full speed ahead toward Ursus Head, Ursus Cove, Bruin Bay.

We were in bear country even bear-ier than the bear country we were leaving. Bears can easily swim to little islands a mile or two from shore, like Scott Island. They can likewise handle swims into sea arches in water too rough for us to paddle, as they might scramble down an almost-cliff that connects one of our pocket beach campsites to the land—on a death-defying slope I'd never set foot on. They can do any or all of that, but we camped on Scott Island anyway, because it's just a bit less likely that a bear would happen to be in that particular place in the same twelve hours that we were.

Whoosh! Flappa-flappa . . . Tweedle-dee-dee . . . Whoosha-whoosha. Tweeeeee . . . Flappa . . . Tweedle-dee . . . How could anyone else be asleep? I sat up in my sleeping bag, focusing on those trilling chirps. Hermit thrush, hermit thrush, hermit thrush . . . hermit thrush? Those cheery little songbirds were definitely responsible for most of the singing, but didn't one sound a little more mechanical? And what on earth could have made the person who invented electric anti-bear fences give them a low-battery alarm that sounded like the chirping of a songbird? Where do they think bears live, anyway, that their fence sounds like nothing but wild summer?

Sticking to the coast let us trade mosquitoes for wind, for the most part. I wriggled out barefoot and gave the closest tent stake an extra shove, for good measure, as I swapped a new pair of shiny AA batteries into our mechanical hermit thrush. The moon was blood-red hazy, almost full, dropping little glints of red to reflect off the ruffled water. Must be summer enough for forest fires somewhere. Summer enough for bears.

The bear fence was this: One rounded black brick between the size of a cell phone and a paperback, with two knobs on top—red and black—shrouded in a thick coat of glue we'd added after discovering that rain would cause sparks to arc between them. A loop of shining orange and silver wire, meticulously put away by Hig, because his standards for coiling it were too persnickety for the rest of us. The brick had three red lights, to indicate a live fence, a ground fault, and whether the power was on. It had one giant yellow button labeled PRESS. Each morning, we popped out the two AAs and flipped one backward because "PRESS" could be pressed in a backpack too, and none of us wanted to reach our hands in to that sort of bite.

Setting it up was a bit like cleaning the cat litter, in that you first tried to find a way to convince yourself it didn't need to be done, then tried to convince someone else to do it, before finally giving in and starting to shovel. Setup often involved literal shoveling, piling stones around propped-up driftwood with the blade of a kayak paddle, in order to have posts to attach the wires to. Occasionally setup involved a task beyond the pale of any household chore—eyes squinted closed and wincing prematurely as you reach out with a tentative hand to see if that 900 volts is really working. That usually fell to Hig. But that sort of thing is manly, right? Like sitting in a group of guy friends when one guy brings out a bag of foreign snacks and says, "This is the worst thing I've ever tasted! You have to try it!" and then they all do.

Usually, we don't touch the fence. We trust the lights on the black brick and our series of everyday rituals: Look for a campsite that's less of a bear corridor. Zip the food into oversized "odor-proof" Ziploc bags. String up the fence, set one can of pepper spray by the door and one by the paddle that holds up the center of the tent. Sleep.

We'd started setting up the bear fence at night round about the time we saw the first mosquito, a month or so ago. We went through the ritual on faith for weeks before the first bear track, and another week or so before we saw our first flesh-and-fur bear. Bears were common now, and the fence had taken on a new importance. The mechanical hermit thrush fell silent, replaced by the quiet ticking I couldn't hear at all over the wind. It shrieked and flapped, and I still couldn't sleep. No bear came, but the wind crashed down the tent. The paddle jumped sideways and then fell, the tent pummeled my head, and when morning finally came, I had an extra cup of coffee. Bears are sexier, and more terrifying, but no bear had yet so much as nosed at our electric fence. Wind and waves were our stolid everyday antagonists.

The pepper spray was the only thing I kept with me. Hig tied my raft to his and let the warm wind pouring out of the bay send both boats sailing down the coast, while Katmai sprinted out his four-year-old wiggles on the sand. I ran behind him. Belemnite fossils blurred past in the rocks. The pepper spray, looped on a strap around my shoulder, thwacked my belly rhythmically with every step. Our prints—my craters, Katmai's dips—pounded across the bear tracks.

One mom, two cubs, probably yearlings, had passed by within a day or so, going our direction. A bear's hind print looks like nothing so much as an oversized human one, with the addition of a set of wicked front claws. My foot landed neatly inside mama's hind print. My next step blurred out the front foot of a baby. The babies' tracks wandered and crisscrossed over mama's more efficient path. How much coaxing does a mother bear do?

We stopped running. The bears' tracks disappeared as we clambered onto the boulder pile where Ursus Head jutted into the sea. Katmai threw "asteroids" into the water, and then the cliffs threw more "asteroids" from above, and I waved my arms toward Hig. Bring the boats back. Pepper spray won't protect us from tumbling rocks. I clipped Katmai's life vest and plopped him into Hig's boat, watching as a fishing line tied to a stick strung out behind them. I followed in my own boat. We caught up with Niki and Lituya about ten minutes later—Katmai practically leaping out of the raft in his eagerness to talk. He launched into a story that would soon transform into a practiced, sing-song repetition.

"Daddy was fishing and fishing, and the only thing he caught was a giant boulder. And then I got into the boat, and I said, 'Can I fish?' And as soon as I grabbed the line I yelled, 'I caught a fish!' And Daddy didn't believe me and then he saw the line move and he said, 'You did catch a fish!' And we pulled it in and Daddy tied a string through its gills, and it was a halibut AS BIG AS MOMMY'S WHOLE LAP." The halibut was sprawled out across my legs, and its tail flopped spastically against my waistband, emphasizing Katmai's point. Its ten or fifteen pounds was a soft wet weight, and its mouth gaped open as it suffocated on my lap. It felt good to grab food from the world. It felt bearlike.

We were kind of like the bears, most of the time, munching our way through the shoreline's most convenient snacks. Maybe we didn't eat the rye grass, or the sand fleas that hopped out of piles of rotten seaweed, but we spiked some meals with the pointed cones of limpets. You can pick out most of the shells from your noodles. Spit out the rest. I peeled leathery nori off the rocks and added that too, probably with a few crunches of sand, and we nearly always plucked the sprigs of petrushki (lovage) that grew in the rocks above the tide line. It tasted like parsley. We ate oyster leaf. Beach spinach. Nettles when we could find them. Fish when we could catch them—less often than I'd like. My kids rolled off logs into the thick cushion of beach greens that grew on the sand and gravel, green juice dripping down their chins as they tore off leaves with baby-white teeth. The additions made even the processed instant whatever-it-is in our packs taste alive.

Fog cut the tops off the mountains and settled on the reefs. A hundred yards stretched into a mile, each row of rocks grayer and mistier than the last. The bottom halves of waterfalls poured into view. On the misty bluffs a boulder shifted. It raised its head. It had a perfect teddy bear nose and perfect teddy bear ears, which were round and fuzzy and framed a brief flash of surprise. Then a perfect round teddy bear rump, jiggling in haste as it retreated into the clouds. Despite the impassible distance of cliffs and water, the bear was frightened of three tiny rubber boats. Good. That's how I like them.

We paddled a lot. Paddling's faster when the wind's at our backs, and even when it isn't, because packrafts may be the slowest boats around, but a four-year-old is even slower. But four-year-olds get antsy, cooped up. So we split the difference. Four of the five of us would walk, and one adult would paddle a raft tied to a raft tied to a raft, with packs and gear and extra paddles heaped up in the caboose. Katmai the paleontologist named the shell shards in the cliff. "That's a googoobudda—it's an ancestor of clams." Lituya toddled along, grubby hands caressing every-thing at a two-foot height. "Look! I see more fossils! And more and more!"

Hig pulled the packraft train onto shore at lunchtime. I broke a few dead alder twigs. Niki grabbed some driftwood. The kids stacked rocks in short but teetering castles. I ran errands back and forth along the line of boulders between our lunch fire and the rafts, barnacles crunching beneath my feet as I grabbed the bag of rice, then the spices, then went back for our bowls . . .

Bears! This mother-yearling pair had brownish-yellowish fur that blended right in to the brownish-yellowish popweed, until it didn't, because bears are far too big to blend into seaweed. Once you notice them. I'd left the pepper spray by the fire and eyed them nervously as I backed slowly up the beach. They eyed me nervously, galloping past within claw-ripping distance of our rafts. The bear and I were both mothers. Neither of us wanted any trouble.

They were gorgeous. Hours later, they were even more gorgeous, slowly climbing a grassy hill as the gold light of evening glinted on their fur. Bears are beautiful. But not quite so beautiful as a common lupine. Bears are agile—galloping up cliff bands with muscles rippling beneath their fur. But not quite so agile as a raven's acrobatics in a storm. Bears are large. Just, large.

Hig balanced the paddle in his left hand, right hand holding our camera up to his eye. He clicked quickly, as the raft spun him away from the shot. "I like seeing bears because they're a sign of a healthy ecosystem."

"I like seeing bears when I'm this far away," I said.

It takes a lot of space to hold a brown bear. They were once thick in Europe, in lands that have long since transformed into cities and farms. The Lower 48 boasts around fifteen hundred of them (also known as grizzlies). The state of Alaska estimates that Game Management Unit 9, where we were currently paddling, has somewhere around six thousand to seven thousand brown bears, with another two thousand to twenty-five hundred in the refuges and parks. That's somewhere around one bear every 3.5 square miles, if they spread themselves out evenly. But bears cluster along salmon streams, coastal sedge plains, and the drift line on the beach, where there are far more than one in 3.5 square miles. The few people in western Cook Inlet also cluster along the coast. The bears easily outnumber us.

Coastal brown bears can grow to well over a thousand pounds on their diet rich in salmon. They're the largest land-based predators, depending on whether you're counting polar bears as land-based, and you'd be forgiven for thinking of them as the top of the food chain. The high spring tides that had driven us out of the sea arch camp had left beaches decked with tangled ropes of kelp and scraps of smaller seaweeds. Bears ate them. Bears grazed the piles as they rotted to goo—swallowing pounds of jumping sand fleas and leaving scat decorated with sharp-edged pumice stones that only a bear's digestive tract could love.

Bears are detritus feeders. Bears are herbivores, grazing salty shore meadows of lyngby's sedge like a herd of furry cows. Bears are fish eaters, and even as we tried to give their fishing holes a wide berth, groups of tourists were flying in every few days to a camp just down the coast, inching as close as they were allowed, trying to replicate the picture of a salmon jumping into a sharp-jawed mouth. Bears are carnivores, and Alaska wildlife officials spend a good deal of effort trying to kill the bears that kill the cute knobbly-kneed baby moose that people would like to eat themselves. Bears dig ground squirrels and clams from their holes and swallow both like candies. Bears are even cannibals. They eat cubs, and in bear-dense areas, the mother bears are trying as hard to avoid the big males as we are, sometimes fleeing right to the tops of snowy barren peaks. All along Kamishak Bay, a thick tangle of alders ensnared the hills, and the tunnels beneath them were traveled by no one but the ursine. Bears are everywhere and eat everything, kind of like Lituya, who'd already consumed a handful of seaweed, a few pebbles, and some fish egg–pattern lures washed up on the beach this afternoon.

The next bear had its nose in a fragrant mess of seaweed. We would have graciously given it the beach it was standing on, if we hadn't had such a long paddle already. Niki and I both really had to pee. Lituya was hungry, but after she'd tossed a water bottle, sunglasses, and a bag of granola bars into the ocean, she'd lost her stuff-in-boat privileges for the day. I paddled in awkward circles to retrieve it all, huffing the same impatient sigh as every parent who's ever bent over to pick up a carrot that went over the side of the high chair. So we picked the end of the beach farthest from the bear's lunch and scrambled out into the small sloppy waves. The bear ran.

Thirty-six hours later, we were still there. I stretched out my legs then crossed them. Lituya sat on my lap then crawled off, grabbed the paddle that held up the tent, and stomped enthusiastically in the one foot of free space she had available. "Go, Lituya! We need a sun dance."

The eight-foot square of gravel beneath our tent was mostly dry. All the other gravel was wet. Rain blew in sheets against the tent walls. The hollering wind dumped rain from five-gallon buckets. It spattered and splattered and shook, and we didn't know what it was doing most of the time, because no one went outside unless they really needed to. Coming in, you had to carefully rebury the edge of the nylon with gravel. We buried dirty compostable diapers in the gravel as well. Niki crowded in with us, and we sat all day, crossing and uncrossing our legs.

Halfway through the afternoon, Lituya crawled on my lap for a nap, and I read the entirety of Niki's pulp mystery novel, minus the first three chapters she'd already burned. The murderer turned out to be the guy you never expected, except of course you expected it all along. It was still raining. It was still much too early to go to sleep. The tent was still small. I smoothed out one of the crumpled pages of Katmai's intertidal guide and reidentified all the sponges. The beach turned to jelly and the poles holding up the electric fence sagged, and the wires drooped and the fence bleated out its sad "ground fault" tune. We decided not to care. Wherever that seaweed-eating bear was, I hoped he had a shelter in the storm at least as good as ours. Perhaps a cave or a worn-down patch of dirt beneath a tunnel of alders. Bears in Kamishak Bay are used to bad weather. They know where to go.

The future promised fifteen-knot winds, eleven-foot seas, rain. But compared to the past (gale warning, thirty-five-knot winds, rain), it seemed good enough. The kids disagreed on the weather. After napping for the first hour or so, Lituya proceeded to yell, "Too windy! Too rainy! I don't want it to be windy and rainy!" Katmai countered with "I like the wind and the rain! I love them!"

Shards of wind-tossed rock were scattered into the meadows of heather, nestled into the leaves of dwarf willows. Dwarf willow leaves grow lower than their roots, because the wind blasts the dirt out from under them, as each new branch clings to the ground. We followed a cliff edge, hundreds of feet above the beach, but shreds of seaweed blew and rolled beside us. The bear trail hugged the precipitous edge. We waded in the grass.

The hills were yellow-green grass, shot through with the purple gray of leafless trunks, of dead and dying alder thickets. We camped in one, in a small grassy space between the arcing curves of branches that crumbled and broke in our hands. The wind died. The golden crowned sparrows sang their three-note lament, and I gathered the drips from the tent until the pot was full enough to burble on Hig's fire of damp rotting alder. It was hard to feel the weight of the alders' loss.

Humans are judgmental nature-lovers. Forests are grand and stately, the sweep of an open grassland is breathtaking, and the blue-white faces of glaciers inspire awe. But it's kind of hard to love a thicket. I've heard of someone who missed alders and went so far as to transplant the shrubs from their home village to the grassy slopes of the Aleutian Islands. Hig tells me about the childhood days he and his sister spent playing "don't touch ground" on those twisted trunks. But most adults? We like to get places. We aren't too fond of crawling, and we *are* fond of views that extend farther than the space we can force open with outstretched arms. Even thicket-loving moose skirt around alders when they have another option. Willows taste better.

The spruce bark beetle marched across the Kenai Peninsula decades ago, and everybody cared when those forests started to die around them. Insects—Bruce's spanworm and the geometrid moths—chewed holes in salmonberry and blueberry leaves at home a few years back, and some people cared. They ate alders too, those caterpillars that turned into a late fall swarm of brown moths around our porch light. But the berries recovered, and I hadn't seen many of those moths around lately. The stripes of dead alder still visible on distant mountainsides—the ones that never recovered—aren't in places that anyone bothers to go.

Alders crumbled dead in the grass, and I wondered if anyone knew why. There were also sick alders with leaves curled into the bedrooms of leaf-rollers. Others looked perfectly normal. There were miles and miles of country where the dominant plant seemed so decimated it wasn't likely to come back—alder thickets turning to grassland. No one we asked could tell us why it had happened, or what it might mean. Alders can colonize new ground. They fix nitrogen into the soil that other plants can use to grow, and the nitrogen seeps into streams to feed whole aquatic ecosystems. They are as useful as the mosquitoes that pollinate the flowers—and as hated. But scientists are spread few and far between out here, busy with the bears and the fish.

Katmai climbed as a bear, in the cratered steps left by the bears that came before us. He climbed as a ground squirrel, scrambling over rocks and slopes. Then he paused, crouched down, nose almost touching the moth that he'd found. It wasn't an alder-eating geometrid. The moths on this hill were gray with orange spots, and they rested with their wings splayed across the tundra, immobile even as we crept up to take their portraits, each one displaying a slightly different pattern than the last.

Maybe Katmai would be a moth next. Or a raven, riding the swirls of a storm. With children, you walk in a world both real and imaginary, and you quickly learn that "Don't you see, Mom?" refers half the time to something no grownup could see. It works well to travel that way. Katmai could always imagine himself into something more wonderful. He could imagine himself, at every storm, and obstacle, into something better adapted for this world. Our detour from sea level had ended, returning us to the beach, where the weather's detour into calm had likewise ended. Wind snorted down the beach, whipping the ocean into lines of breaking white. The air tasted salty. It was damp, and heavy, pushing against us.

In 1890, Robert Porter called Kamishak Bay—this broad swath of coastline that extended from Harriet Point to Cape Douglas—the Forgotten Shore. "All through the winter the shores of the Kamishak are deserted and desolate," he wrote, "a wilderness of barren rock and drifting snow, the battlefield of furious gales, and trembling before the unceasing onslaught of a raging sea, kept in a state of turmoil by the joint action of wind and tide." No wonder it's such a good place for bears. For ground squirrels and marmots and all the creatures that sleep through the dark and see this place only in the brief few months of summer. They crawl out onto Kamishak's beaches right about when the grass is sprouting and the fish and people are migrating back.

Native people didn't stay the winter either, and the few white hunters who did anchored their camps to the rocks with heavy chains. Years ago, Hig and I had passed through the howling winds and thick salt ice only briefly. It was good that we had seen it in winter, or I'd be thinking Kamishak was a pretty tough place in July. Kamishak Bay is less mountainous than most of this coast. Wind notices this. Wind funnels through that low, unremarkable piece of land, from Cook Inlet to Lake Iliamna to Bristol Bay beyond. Or the other way around. This is a door between the Gulf of Alaska and the Bering Sea.

We strolled into the salt spray, picking up fossils. Tiny clam shells like white waves frozen inside pebbles, long round belemnite cylinders, bivalves fluted like fans. We kicked "tsunami buoys"—big oblong aquaculture buoys in black or orange that had likely washed here from Japan's 2011 disaster. Hig counted fifteen. We picked up a toy wheel. A contact lens case with a gooseneck barnacle on one side and an "L" on the other that spurred Lituya to claim it as her own. The wind scoured the land and the waves crashed against the rocks, bringing an ocean of trash and wood and shells. Katmai collected the drift in armfuls, dragging the end of a scrub brush through the sand. Dozens of orange foam basketballs wedged themselves in cracks between the driftwood logs.

The scat at the top of the beach told us that the bears, at this time of the year, were mostly eating plants. We were mostly eating pecans and pretzel crumbs and the last two granola bars—the only snacks we had to take us to the camp at the McNeil River Wildlife Sanctuary. A pair of bears, likely siblings, rounded the corner of a barnacle-studded cliff. They watched us. Our camp was still set up, and we stood together in the tiny square created by our bear fence and watched them back, until they finally turned around.

For the fish, each day of wind and rain added up to as much summer as any day of sun. Fishermen can get them as soon as they draw near to shore, but the bears have to wait for that final spawning run up a creek, where the fish had only just begun to arrive. Salmon leapt into the air in the shallows of Chenik Creek, just around a few rocky points from our camp, where those bears had been coming from.

We were nearly in the wildlife sanctuary. The ocean would carry us there. Waves shoaled on the reef, whipped up into long hissing breakers we had to paddle half a mile to sea to avoid. Even there, the reef was so shallow that my paddle tip grazed the bottom of the sea. The wind pushed us up the bay, past knobbly cliffs and a skylight hole where you might fall right from the tundra into the waves. We passed a huge boulder cracked into three tilted slices, and the litter of young marmots that cowered in the cliffs behind it. We paddled into a flock of hundreds of sea ducks, who struggled to lift off as their fat bellies smacked the waves with every flap.

The wind pushed us to a trio of structures that marked the McNeil River camp, and a bear standing idly on the beach in front of them. I glowered at it. Bears were the point, of course. If you approach a village from the wilderness, you tend to see a gradual diminishing of bear sign, until all the tracks disappear at an invisible line that both people and bears seem to know. Bears aren't welcome in most human communities, and they usually get shot when they draw near, but a bear sanctuary camp was created for an entirely opposite purpose. As many as 144 different individual bears may visit McNeil River in the summer. Up to seventy-four have been seen at one time, which is proudly noted on the state website that tells you how you can apply for the lottery to come watch them.

The bear finally moved out of the way, and we made our way up to camp, where we were surrounded by ten overjoyed photographers, discussing the fishing techniques of diving bears, the nicknames of particular bears, and f-stops and lenses that could best capture this extraordinary spectacle. They slept in tents and paid far less than the guests at Silver Salmon Creek Lodge, but these people had waited years to win this chance to walk a certain path to a certain spot, guided by rangers, to watch the crowds of bears. I told them all the bears we'd seen so far had been polite. They had seen more bears in a handful of days than we had in three months, and "politeness" is not how they were thinking about the wildlife. We hadn't won the bear-viewing lottery, however, so we weren't allowed to walk up that creek. But even in camp, looking out at the beaches, there were bears enough for me.

The lottery I'd won was the lottery of family. A husband interested in the same crazy trips I was, all four of us physically healthy and not dragged down by any particular misfortune. We had enough luck that we could make our own, living cheaply and piecing together digital contract work that gave us the freedom to be out here in the wild. Out here, I didn't want to depend on luck. Not on lotteries and not on the whims and personalities of particular bears.

Parenthood has made me more curmudgeonly toward other mammals. It has made me less patient with enthusiastically ill-behaved dogs that snatch food from babies and rush toward oncoming cars—because don't I have enough irresponsible little creatures to care for already? Parenthood makes me less enamored of bears. A bite from a brown bear could easily crush my skull. It could even more easily crush a child's. It's different when you're a mom. The predators loom larger, the waves look taller—every risk is supersized next to the diminutive body of your own small child. Mother bears feel the same tension. They kill more humans than any other bears—more than the large males ever do—but far fewer than the number of bears killed by humans. Bears are an amazing part of the wilderness. Still, I hoped there wasn't one around the next corner.

Sometimes you're too immersed in the wilderness to see it. The tourists at McNeil could watch the bears with unblemished joy because they existed in a thin bubble where they didn't need to interact with bears. The bubble was entirely virtual, and it had been constructed carefully by the rangers over many years, leading groups of tourists along the same well-worn paths to the same well-worn watching spots until the humans became nothing but a picture on the wall. They built a bubble of trust where the bears don't startle anymore. Where the bears don't care and the people pointing their cameras at them can wonder, "How is this bear interacting with the world?" rather than, "How will this bear interact with my family?"

We ate dinner with Tom and his colleagues inside the ranger's cabin, where he'd lived for fourteen summers watching tourists and bears. An old male bear ambled by out the window, and Tom recounted his lengthy history of courtships and misadventures. Suddenly, that bear seemed more animal to me. I started to warm to the idea of that bubble. You could see the bears better from inside it. They were less scary here, and losing that fear made them seem more real—more three-dimensional. I wondered what the chances were of getting myself into that lottery someday. Tom walked us down the coast when we left the camp. The beach is the only place he'll walk, that and the tiny patch of grassland around the cluster of buildings and tents. Decades ago a trash fire had gone astray, and the alder had never returned. Everywhere else was brush-tunnel bear trails, and Tom considered it too dangerous to walk where you couldn't see.

Conglomerate boulders littered the shore where they'd tumbled from McNeil Head. Tom clapped at every one of them. *Clap-Clap! Clap-Clap!* He clapped at every boulder, every cliff, at any possible spot a bear could sit unseen. "Just letting them know I'm here." *Clap-Clap! Clap-Clap!* He asked us about packrafts. We talked about moths and marmots, about ecosystem shifts and acidifying oceans. He talked right over the claps. Didn't break stride. When Tom turned and left us after a lunch on the sunny shore, I tried to remember to clap at the next clump of boulders.

Because bears are an amazing part of the wilderness. And there might be one around that next corner.

Lituya clutches the greenling she caught in Sukoi Bay, where Cook Inlet ends and Shelikoff Strait begins.

ENDINGS

There are several different ways to become an expert. Some of them involve years of careful study. Some of them involve degrees and classes and apprenticeships and learning from masters of the trade. But some do not. Sometimes, you're an expert in something just because no one else was genius enough or stupid enough to do it before you, and you're stuck with all the joys of a self-invented specialty. Hig and I were possibly the world experts in ocean packrafting.

Not expert packrafters, which would require an ability to read rapids, quickly navigate around holes, and shoot down waterfalls that make me tremble just watching the clips on YouTube. Not expert ocean paddlers, which would require an ability to roll a kayak, shoot through lines of curling surf, and ride storm-tossed seas twenty or fifty miles from any shore. Nope. We were just the only people who'd even considered paddling more than a thousand miles of flat water in tiny, slow, single-chamber vessels with zero tracking ability, and less than zero ability to slice through oncoming surf.

The surf was coming. The tide was rising. Tom had snapped a family photo and waved goodbye as he hiked back to camp, clapping at every rock. We scurried between piles and heaps and sacks of gear. Stuffed things in packs, clipped life vests, popped-together kayak paddles, rolled-shut drybags, and zipped-shut snack bags. An unspoken worry urged us adults onward, a constant nagging voice that whispered, "The launching spots are disappearing! The launching spots are disappearing!" I'd seen it happen too often. Rafts half-inflated, kids half-ready, and then the tide creeps over that rock that was breaking the swell, and that tiny kink in the coastline that used to be a harbor—that promised an escape—is gone.

Water surged around the scatter of boulders, tumbled here from McNeil Head above us. Niki was quickest off the beach. I watched her bobbing down the coast, up and down and up and down—a shrinking yellow bubble on the rolling lines of waves that surged toward shore. Should we even be here? I wanted to yell out "How's the water?!" but she was too far to hear. Waves wrapped around a tiny rock, leaving just enough space for a raft.

"Hig, lift Lituya in for me!" He and Katmai followed quickly. "I think this is a bad idea!" I yelled, nearly as soon as I'd left the shore. The waves arched up, breaking white around us.

"It might be a little wet, but it should be much better when we get around this point!" The doubts that plague the rest of us rarely bother Hig.

"I don't think we're getting around the point!" I yelled back.

"This isn't a good place to land!" Hig argued.

"It'll have to be!"

A wave broke beneath the bow of Niki's boat, where she was facing out to sea, waiting for us. It picked her up, tossed her upside-down in the lines of rolling breakers on the shoal.

"Are you okay?!" I called out. I couldn't hear her answer. She was swimming now, life vest and head above the breakers, raft pulling behind her. Why didn't she get in the boat? Hig paddled closer, maybe plotting some kind of help. I nudged closer as well, a trick while trying to keep the boat angled perfectly perpendicular to the waves. The kids watched from our boats, unperturbed. To them, a capsize was a mistake to laugh about later, as long as it wasn't them getting dunked.

"I'm fine!" she repeated, once we were close enough to hear. "I can touch bottom here!"

The bottom was barely beneath us, and its nearness steepened the waves into the breaking whitecapped mess that was causing us such trouble. I tried to surf the swells in. Keep perpendicular to the waves and ride them onto the gravel. Easy does it. Pick a smallish set of waves. Only feet from shore now. One last line of breaks. Almost there.

Splash! A whirl of white, gray, wet, knees thumping on sand then standing up and grasping for everything. I plucked Lituya from where she floated next to me in her life vest, yelling at the indignity of it all. I grabbed the paddle in my other hand, and dragged the heavy water-filled raft along a line behind it. The water was knee-deep. I walked up the beach.

I must have been angled to the waves. Just a tiny angle, but enough to catch the pointed stern of the raft and flip me over back to front. I thought I had aimed better than that. But it all went so quickly. So quickly that my hair never even got wet. So quickly that I never felt scared. Maybe Hig was right to be confident, as he was the only one who managed to land without a dunking. I dripped beside the fire. We had gotten only a few hundred yards from the launch spot. It couldn't be counted as progress, but I guess the beach where we'd landed was as good a beach as the one we'd started on. Katmai crowed about being the only one not to tip over on this expedition, and Lituya dried out, and I sat down beside them, building rock castles. Socks and diapers waved gently on a string stretched between the fire and the cliffs.

Losses tallied: One extra pair of sunglasses. One glove. One camera lens, possibly recoverable. A dollop of confidence. A tablespoon of morale. "I think we should do a final check before we launch next time." The other adults nodded their agreement. "You know, to make sure it's still a good idea."

We'd gotten so caught up in the idea that we had to launch because the launch spots were disappearing, rushing around in a heads-down hurry that blinded us to the even more basic fact that the *calm water* was disappearing as well. We rolled the experience around between us for another half hour, tossing it back and forth, examining all sides, then tucking it away. One more pebble of wisdom to add to the collection in our pockets, for next time.

Everyone else bailed to the tents when it rained. I ducked under a tiny overhang, contorting to keep my nose out of the fire smoke and my head out of the rain. Spatters of rain blew on my feet, and stray drops beaded up on my waterproof notebook as I dutifully scratched down the day's misadventures in half-legible pencil scrawl, starting with page 376. Pages 1–250 had been mailed away a long time ago. We'd started in winter and now it was July, and even the written weight of all the experiences in between would be too heavy to carry. A curl of wind drifted the smoke across my rock and I escaped to the water's edge, watching rain pelt the waves. I missed the tent with the wood stove. This was Kamishak Bay, where the air drops its rain as it sweeps between Cook Inlet and Bristol Bay. Maybe a winter tent is called for in July.

The next morning, drizzle glued the beach to us. Sheets of sand shed from the kids' coats as they wrestled. Low tide swept the ocean away from our beach, and we crunched over barnacles, cobblestone, and popweed. We walked half a mile to sea, then half a mile more in ankle-deep water, until we could paddle in water that had transformed into something as flat as the sand.

Lituya munched potato chips in a soothing rhythm, lying back to crunch with her eyes closed until she finally fell asleep, her soggy crumb-covered hand still curled as if to grasp an invisible chip from a now-removed bag. Her face shone with safflower oil, and the rain spread slick across her freckled cheeks. The rain didn't bead up on our clothing anymore. It trickled in through the tattered pores as if there wasn't really anything left between us and the world. It soaked into our sleeves with each stroke of the paddle, and washed our grime into a swirling brown puddle at the bottom of the boat.

It took a bonfire to make us human again. The flames leapt to meet the drops, steaming the knees of our rainpants until they were too hot to touch and the heat started to flicker into our boat-stiff legs. Rolls of rotted seaweed built a rich soil at the top of the beach, where a waterfall spattered on the sand. We ate wilted beach spinach and wild sorrel on noodles. It didn't look as fancy as it tasted, but it tasted amazing. Amphipods leapt into the fire, cooking themselves into shrimpy pink curls, and when the gravel had cooled to a gentle warmth, we set the tent right on top of it. We slept on a heated floor of pebbles and fire-crisped amphipods. Rocks clattered from the cliffs up the bay.

The stream went *glug-shoosh*, the bear fence went *tick-tick-tick,* and the amphipods that hadn't been killed leapt at the tent fabric like a steady rain. *Pop-skitter-slide, pop-skitter-slide, pop-skitter-slide,* all night long.

"I like home better than this trip," Katmai commented, stirring his bowl of rice-and-petrushki-and-a-little-bit-of-sand. "I like this trip a lot, but I like home better."

It was me who'd started it. I was done with my bowl of rice, and I'd just been going on about the pies and breads and pizzas I'd make when I got home. The wet crunch of fresh kohlrabi slices, the deep green leather of kale. Would there be any radishes still in the ground? No excuse to long for food now. We were moving fast. Miles of water slid past on every calm day, and that speed more than made up for the storms. Our food bags were still satisfyingly heavy. But what would it feel like to take a bite of a dinner that hadn't been boiled?

I still hiked with Tyrannosaurs sometimes. But more often, the kids traveled in imaginary airplanes. Real Cessnas were an occasional buzz in the air out here. We'd seen them so close to cliffs I'd worried for the pilots' safety. I'd scuffed their tire tracks on the beach and shuffled through the remains of the pilots' clam-feed picnic. But the imaginary planes seemed built of candy sugar and a vague memory of an interstate flight, and they soon grew into ungainly beasts that would guzzle fuel as they lifted their ice-cream factories and pizza ovens into the sky.

After three and a half months, Cape Douglas was finally looming above us. Glaciers grew on the wimpy volcano like a scaly blue-white rash, spilling over the valleys in a solid proof that it was usually wet here. Mount Douglas still held onto hundreds of years of snow. It swept up from the bear-studded sedge flats to fill half the sky. We'd been aiming for Douglas for so long. The bulk of that peak made it impossible not to think about the end of things.

When we were packing to leave McNeil, one of the rangers asked how we managed to drag ourselves away—to keep on going beyond the warm dry havens along the way. Stepping out the door, I gave a flippant answer: "I'm excited to see what's coming next." True, but I'm also a slave to ambition—buoyed by the pride and satisfaction of seeing an enormous goal through to completion and fearing the shameful tinge of failure. I'm following my own grand plan, tackling obstacles, striving for success, just like writing a book, starting a business, running a marathon, or any one of the sparkling challenges humans set for themselves.

Yet most of the time, I'm not even doing that. Most of the time, my thoughts are ordinary and unambitious, even in the wilderness. Most of the time, I'm trudging one foot in front of the other, doing exactly what most of us do.

I do what I did yesterday. That's usually what I do, what you do, what nearly everybody does. Maybe you eat something different for breakfast, or pull up a different document on the computer, or have a different patient in the operating room, or lay the roofing on a different house, or climb a different mountain. So what? We are all fundamentally ordinary, whatever our ordinary is. And even as my paddles spin to brace against a wave, and my feet dance from boulder to boulder, and a bear suddenly appears against the sunset, all that stuttering breathtaking change adds up to something as rhythmic as our five beating hearts.

In less than a week, that rhythm would stop.

"I want a house on this island."

"You don't," Hig replied.

"No, I don't." I spun the camera past the gold-washed cliffs and the pink-yellow smash of sunset on glacial crevasses. "I don't. But I guess when I say that, I mean I just want to know this place better." The beach cobbles broke into curls of ammonite fossils, the grazing bears were like golden haystacks on a field of green, and when the sun lit low across the lupine and paintbrush, I couldn't quite believe I'd ever climb into one of those little bush airplanes—buzzing off like our friend Bjorn had just a few hours ago.

He was a bear-viewing guide, but I'd mistaken him for a bear. Bjorn only wears black, and what else moves out here? He had just a minute to snap a picture of his own—his shift over and the pilot waiting—before introducing us to his fellow guide and a pair of Swiss guests. No cabins here. Their tents were a cross between what you might bring car camping and what you might set up at a street fair, perched in the middle of a careful house-sized rectangle of triple-strand electric fence.

These were the last people beyond McNeil's bear-viewing camp. The only possible people we could ask our question: What is the future? In thickly accented English, the Swiss man who'd barely seen Alaska told us that he hoped Alaska could keep what it has—all its wild places and wildlife—because Europe had lost all that such a long time ago and you can never go back.

Looking over the sweep of bears and glaciers, what other answer could you expect? Everyone knows Alaska is special. Even the newest Alaskans cling to what they came for. Big fish, big mountains, big dreams, and the stubborn differentness of anyone who would call most of their own country "Outside." We fear it will end up like everywhere else.

The dropping tide left our Jurassic island perched in glistening ripples of sand. Salt rings on our clothes, salt stinging my nose. Glittering puddles. The sound of small feet puddle splashing was like the sound of any kid, except when else does Mom let you walk through water for half a mile in your sneakers? We splashed through channels and then climbed the piles of buoys tossed like party balloons on the top of the beach.

The beach grew to gravel. Then cobbles. Then boulders, piling against the shore until the last one stood by the edge of a ragged sandstone cliff and we sat down on top of it, pulling out the snacks. "It's steeper on the other side," Hig reported, breathless, skate-sliding down from above us. "I'll take the packs first. Then Katmai."

Dust flew. Butts red-brown and worn down, scraping every flapping cuff and worn thread of our pants through a crumbled-steep chute that wasn't a trail but it was the way the bears went, almost a gully, and the footing wasn't bad if you remembered not to look down. I forgot. I looked down. The ocean was shiny in the sun and whipped into the waves that had stopped us from paddling around the cliffs. It was not as close as I'd like it to be. I've always been afraid of heights. I cursed at the steep trail but removed the curse words for the benefit of the two-year-old listening over my shoulder. Lituya had picked up my tension, whining continuously into my ear. I clutched the shattered red rock with white knuckles and slowed to the speed of the rock-grabbing limpet I was pretending to be. Katmai and Hig proceeded cheerily along ahead of us, hand in hand. Hig wasn't afraid of heights, and Katmai was still young enough to trust Daddy absolutely.

"Steeper on the other side!?" Niki exclaimed. It was an egregious example of Hig's tendency to understate difficulties, and we ribbed him for it at the bottom of the chute, building rock castles with the kids. The stones were flat and warm in my palm. I poured a handful of them into Lituya's outstretched hand, payment for a plate of imaginary fruit. We played, we forgave, we paddled.

Read about adventures and you'll read about the conflict of expedition partners—about clashing egos and broken teams and weather-frayed nerves setting people lashing out at their teammates. I'd take my family over any of them. Because each of us, even our two-year-old, has something that can never be matched by technical skills or physical strength. Comfort in the wilderness. Comfort with each other.

A fox paced the shore, its orange fur a perfect match for Lituya's tousled hair. Harlequin ducks swam in a flapping chaos through a sea arch. It was easy to pretend that we were the only humans in the world. If there were more, they must not know how beautiful it is out here. If anyone knew how beautiful it was, they would be here.

At camp, Katmai practiced his balance on a drifted-up soccer ball, and we rolled a buoy as big as a car to block the wind from one side of Niki's tent. Every few minutes, a gust would roar through from an unpredictable direction, straining the tent fabric, sending us scattering for more logs and rocks to weigh down each corner. Katmai led Lituya to a patch of petrushki and carefully showed her the right plant to eat. In between gusts we hunted leaf fossils.

We do the same thing every day. Ordinary, and childish. Out here, I feel more like a kid. I play in the mud and I build things with pebbles, but I feel like a kid because this world is so intense. Because I live in the moment here. I feel the storms, the wind, the cliffs, the beauty. It's easy to be overwhelmed by both the negatives and the positives, seesawing back and forth between them sometimes a half-dozen times in a day. There's the despair of storms and waves, and weary grumping that nothing will ever feel warm and dry again. Then the sun breaks through, or a sea lion gives us a show, and I feel like I could do this forever. That we should just keep going, around the next bay and the next, tracing the whole coast of Alaska for however many years it takes. Or at least plan another trip just like this, next time.

That's what softens the ending. There's always a next time.

On the second to last day, we turned the corner. Kodiak Island hunched in a blue haze, our new view across the water. Kodiak wasn't burning, but somewhere inland, it was, sending tiny soot particles drifting out across the clear summer sky. We didn't know to expect the dropping tide current in Shelikoff Strait to shove against us. We weren't in Cook Inlet anymore. The imaginary line had been crossed. We could go home anytime.

Lituya, with Hig's help, caught a small kelp greenling in the mirror pool of Sukoi Bay. Her fish story of the trip, to mirror her brother's. She'd be too young to remember it for long, but every kid needs their tiny family legends. A pair of male bears chased each other in pursuit of a female on the hills above us, light and dark splotches on a backdrop of iris and lupine and *pushki* (cow parsnip) meadow. Another appeared at the edge of a small channel where we cooked lunch, wading neck deep to cool off, then lumbering, dripping, up to graze on the far shore. I was less nervous than I'd been a month earlier. Every bear out here had been as polite to us as we tried to be to them.

Bears act differently in different parts of the state. I believe they have cultures. Mashups between their biology and their particular environment, passed down from mom to cub. The nervous Arctic bears looking over their shoulders as they ran past. The grumpy tension of Unimak Island bears. These Cook Inlet bears were targets of bear viewers for a reason. Fat on fish, rubbing shoulders with neighbors, slow-moving and Midwestern polite. I still watched them with pepper spray in hand, but the bears' relaxed attitude had rubbed off on me too.

We follow in bears' footprints. But humans' prints can be more mysterious. A parked skiff, tucked into a landing on the protected side of a spit, pulled up onto the beach with bear-proof food containers and a well-tied rope. The boot tracks were washed by the tide, walked over by bears, rolled over by wheel tracks. As if someone arrived by skiff and left by plane, in some kind of hurry. I could only guess at that story. Then we paddled away again. I wondered if the sun had made us hurry too much, paddle too much, miss too much that we see when the weather slows us down to a boulder-hopping crawl. The end was rushing up so fast. I told the kids how amazing this was. How proud I was that they came *all the way around Cook Inlet*. They ignored me completely.

As they should. Kids know instinctively that each day is a new adventure and if you string a lot of them together, maybe that's nothing to be proud of. But each day of memories is something to be grateful for. We shied away from the end of those memories. Overshot the first possible landing spot, forcing ourselves to go forward or to retreat against the wind. So we hiked through the fireweed that towered over Katmai's head and paddled to the crumbling edge of Four-Peaked Glacier. A mother brown bear with two dark spring cubs huffed and snorted as she scrambled up the steep bank away from our packrafts, her crap sliding down the polished rock behind her.

At the edges of the lake, ice gave way to stone, then moss, then alder. A glacier's future is simple. Glaciers melt.

I imagined the other futures people had told us, reflected in the turquoise-gray water of the lake. Folks out in wild places worried they'd disappear. Villages growing empty, the sporties winning out over family setnet fishermen, and modern digital humans moving into the cities they belong in—leaving the land to grow lonely. Some people worried that climate change and growing global populations would swamp Alaska with people, the hardscrabble homesteader culture we like to believe in washed out by too many newcomers. Others worried that the oil industry we depend on would die, and take Alaska's people and economy with it. Holding onto what we have was the most people dared to hope for. We heard that hope. But people had seen the crabs and sea birds and king salmon and bidarki and spruce forests and fishermen and elders disappear. We heard that too. No one was sure. Alaskans have a pompous pride in their self-reliance. Maybe we'll need it.

Maybe we're as powerful as glaciers. Taking down mountains. Chiseling the world with the stubborn weight of our convictions. Maybe we're as vulnerable as glaciers. Just an average of the conditions of our place and time, thriving or declining based on the fickle vagaries of climate—real, economic, or political. I know we are at least more flexible than the ice that shatters into crevasses at each curve in the slope.

The kids pulled their boots off and wriggled into the pool. They turned the turquoise to a muddy gray, splashing in a kettle pond the ice had dug out in the gravel beach. They shivered, faces as gray blue as a glacier until the flush of cold was beaten back by the flush of exuberant splashing. They got used to it.

Katmai practiced paddling his own raft, and Lituya was ready to get out of diapers. They were growing up. The future marched on. Every time we'd run into another human on this journey, Katmai had reminded me in an urgent not-whisper to ask them our question. He sat through every adult worry about salmon and oil and oceans that would dissolve the shell of a clam. Then forgot them. My kids are the future of Alaska, and maybe it's best that they won't remember what everyone else warned about it.

Maybe they'll remember that everyone had something to say. Maybe they'll remember that a patch of ground feels different under your sleeping head. That every broken item can be repaired with Spectra thread. That you can heave up your ordinary and live life in an utterly different way, but still be the same old you. That no one with family can ever truly be homesick.

We all hope to bend the future a little for our kids. We also hope they'll get used to it.

Spray flew from the floats as the plane we'd chartered skidded to a halt in front of our beach. The intercom system roared with static as we rose above the sea, cold wind rushing in as Hig opened the window to snap pictures. We reversed the journey of three and a half months in less than an hour and dropped our sleeping bags and notebooks into the yurt we'd left behind. Until the next time.

FURTHER READING

Alaska Department of Natural Resources. *Cook Inlet Areawide Oil and Gas Lease Sale: Final Finding of the Director.* 2009.

Alaska Humanities Forum. *Alaska History and Cultural Studies.* www.akhistorycourse.org.

Bancroft, Hubert. *History of Alaska, 1730–1885.* Originally published 1886. New York: Antiquarian Press, 1959.

Barry, Mary. *A History of Mining on the Kenai Peninsula.* Anchorage: Alaska Northwest Publishing Co., 1973.

Beresford, William. *A Voyage Round the World: But More Particularly to the North-West Coast of America: Performed in 1785, 1786, 1787, and 1788, in the King George and Queen Charlotte.* With an introduction by George Dixon. London: G. Goulding, 1789.

Boraas, Alan. "A Summary of Kenai Peninsula Prehistory," *Kenai River Landowner's Guide.* Edited by Devony Lehner. Homer, AK: US Department of Agriculture, 1992.

Boraas, Alan. "Native Life: One Hundred Years of Native Life on the Kenai Peninsula," *Alaska's Kenai Peninsula: The Road We've Traveled.* Hope, AK: Kenai Peninsula Historical Association, 2002.

Cook, James. *A Voyage to the Pacific Ocean: Undertaken by the Command of His Majesty for Making Discoveries in the Northern Hemisphere Performed under the Direction of Captains Cook, Clerke, and Gore* in the Years 1776, 1777, 1778, and 1780. London: Stockdale, Scatcherd, and Whitaker, 1784.

Davidson, George. *Pacific Coast: Coast Pilot of Alaska (First Part) from Southern Boundary to Cook's Inlet.* US Coast and Geodetic Survey, 1869.

Davis, Nancy Yaw, and William E. Davis, eds. *Adventures Through Time: Readings in the Anthropology of Cook Inlet, Alaska.* Anchorage: Cook Inlet Historical Society, 1996.

De Laguna, Frederica. *The Archaeology of Cook Inlet, Alaska.* 2nd edition. Anchorage: Alaska Historical Society, 1975.

Dickey, William. "The Sushitna River, Alaska." *National Geographic* Vol. 8, pp. 322–327, 1897.

Glenn, Edwin, and William Abercrombie. *Reports of Explorations in the Territory of Alaska (Cooks Inlet, Sushitna, Copper, and Tanana Rivers).* Washington, DC: GPO, 1899.

Haycox, Stephen. *Alaska: An American Colony.* Seattle: UW Press, 2006.

Jones, Suzi, James A. Fall, and Aaron Leggett, eds. *Dena'inaq' Huch'ulyeshi: The Dena'ina Way of Living.* Anchorage: Anchorage Museum, 2013.

Kari, James, et al. *Shem Pete's Alaska: The Territory of the Upper Cook Inlet Dena'ina.* Fairbanks: UA Press, 2003.

Kari, Priscilla Russell. *Tanaina Plantlore: An Ethnobotany of the Dena'ina Indians of Southcentral Alaska.* Fairbanks: Alaska Native Language Center, 1995.

Klein, Janet R. *Kachemak Bay Communities: Their Histories, Their Mysteries.* Homer, AK: Kachemak Country Publications, 2008.

Lloyd, Steve. *Farallon: Shipwreck and Survival on the Alaska Shore.* Pullman: WSU Press, 2000.

Lord, Nancy. *Fish Camp: Life on an Alaskan Shore.* Berkeley: Counterpoint, 2000.

Merritt, Roy D. *Chronicle of Alaska Coal-Mining History.* Fairbanks: Alaska Division of Geological and Geophysical Surveys, 1986.

Osgood, Cornelius. *The Ethnography of the Tanaina.* New Haven, Conn.: Yale University Press, 1937.

Reger, R. D., et al. *A Guide to the Late Quaternary History of Northern and Western Kenai Peninsula, Alaska.* Fairbanks: Alaska Division of Geological and Geophysical Surveys, 2007.

State of Alaska, Department of Labor, Research and Analysis, 1880 Census, 1890 Census, and 1910 Census—supplement for Alaska.

Sweetland, B. S., and R. J. Barnett. *Russian America: The Forgotten Frontier.* Tacoma: Washington State Historical Society, 1990.

Tyonek Native Corporation. "Tyonek: History and Culture." www.tyonek.com/who-we-are/history-culture.

Vancouver, George. *A Voyage of Discovery to the North Pacific Ocean and Round the World.* London: G. G. and J. Robinson, 1798.

Walcott, Charles D. *Annual Reports of the Department of the Interior for the Fiscal Year Ended June 30, 1899.* Washington, DC: GPO, 1900.

Woodward Spring, Susan. *Seldovia, Alaska: An Historical Portrait of Life in Zaliv Seldevoe-Herring Bay.* Littleton, CO: Blue Willow, 1997.

ACKNOWLEDGMENTS

I would like to thank Faith, my most faithful and thorough editor, over every book I've written. Without her help, I wouldn't be acknowledging anyone. Also Valisa, Tim, and Niki, for their advice and edits; Hig, for keeping me honest; and everyone at Mountaineers Books.

A book like this requires thanks not only for my partners in writing, but for my muddy, wet, wave-tossed partners on the journey itself. I thank Hig for being my co-conspirator and partner on every crazy expedition. Katmai, for the imaginative creature sightings that livened all our days and for putting up with parents who expect a four-year-old to walk hundreds of miles in a summer. Lituya, for the giggles in my ear and the mud pancakes. Niki, for introducing me to the wilderness as a child and for her willingness to still get out there with me, many decades later. Erik, for riding the Turnagain tides with us.

I would also like to thank every person who let us dump muddy gear on their floor, borrow a shower, crash a spare room, mail them a food box, share a meal, or enjoy a great conversation. Thank you for putting up with our grubby clothes and tricky questions. There are so many of you, from Nanwalek to Cape Douglas and everywhere in between. You were the backbone of our journey. Without you, the land would be more lonely.

ABOUT THE AUTHOR

Erin McKittrick grew up in Seattle, exploring the wilderness of the nearby Cascade Range. She met her husband, Hig, at Carleton College, where she graduated with a BA in biology in 2001. Erin also has a master's degree in molecular and cellular biology from the University of Washington. After they finished college, Erin and Hig took off on their first major Alaska adventure together, setting them both on a new life path.

Erin is the author of A *Long Trek Home: 4,000 Miles by Boot, Raft, and Ski; Small Feet, Big Land: Adventure, Home, and Family on the Edge of Alaska* (National Outdoor Book Award winner for 2014); and *My Coyote Nose and Ptarmigan Toes: An Almost-True Alaskan Adventure*. She is a regular contributor to the *Alaska Dispatch News* and her writing also appears in a number of other books, magazines, and online outlets. In addition to writing, she works for an environmental consulting firm and helps run a nonprofit organization, Ground Truth Trekking, which combines the "ground truth" of wilderness expeditions with the "researched truth" of science, to shed light on the crucial natural resource issues facing Alaska and the world. Learn more at www.groundtruthtrekking.com.

Erin lives with her husband and two children in Seldovia, Alaska, a four-hundred-person fishing village unconnected to the road system.